TABLE OF CONTENTS

ACRONYMS

CA	Civil Affairs
CGSC	U.S. Army Command and General Staff College
CIA	Central Intelligence Agency
CNN	Cable News Network
DoD	Department of Defense
DoS	Department of State
FBI	Federal Bureau of Investigations
IW	Irregular Warfare
JSOTF	Joint Special Operations Task Force
JSOU	Joint Special Operations University
MMAS	Masters Degree in Military Art and Science
NSA-1947	National Security Act of 1947
NSC	National Security Council
NSS	National Security Staff
OOTW	Operations Other Than War
POLAD	Political Advisor
PSYOP	Psychological Operation
SAMS	School of Advanced Military Studies
SEAL	Navy Sea Air Land teams
SOF	Special Operations Forces
TF	Task Force
UN	United Nations
UNITAF	Unified Task Force
UNOSOM	United Nations Operations in Somalia
UNSCR	United Nations Security Council Resolution
USAFRICOM	United States Africa Command
USSOCOM	United States Special Operations Command

ILLUSTRATIONS

TABLES

INTRODUCTION

The military services are but a part of the national machinery of peace or war. An effective national security policy calls for active, intimate and continuous relationships not alone between the military services themselves but also between the military services and many other departments and agencies of Government.[1]
— Ferdinand Eberstadt to James Forrestal, 1947

Neither we nor the international community has either the responsibility or the means to do whatever it takes for as long as it takes to rebuild nations.[2]
—Tony Lake, U.S. National Security Advisor, March 6, 1996

Americans are amazingly compassionate people. This burden often places the nations' policymakers in difficult situations. Generally, states should not intervene in the domestic affairs of others.[3] The nation's policymakers determine and articulate the justification for intervention to not only the United States domestic audiences, but also to the international community, describing the presumed necessity for intervention. Included in this explanation are the U.S. military objectives along with areas that international partners can assist during the course of

---

[1]David Rothkopf, Running the World: The Inside Story of the National Security Council and the Architects of American Power (New York: Public Affairs, 2005), 52. Ferdinand Eberstadt, a leading attorney and banker in New York responded to a question from his friend James Forrestal, then the Secretary of Navy (and later Secretary of Defense), regarding how to organize the post war World War II military services.

[2]Anthony Lake, "Defining Missions, Setting Deadlines" (prepared remarks to George Washington University, Washington D.C., March 6, 1996), http://www.defense.gov/speeches/speech.aspx?speechid=898 (accessed January 31, 2013).

[3]Thomas G. Weiss, "Overcoming the Somalia Syndrome - "Operation Rekindle Hope?"," Global Governance (1995) http://heinonline.org/HOL/LandingPage?collection=journals&handle=hein.journals/glogo1&div=17&id=&page= (accessed August 12, 2012). Weiss argues that according to post-Vietnam logic, the United States should not intervene unless it is committed to total victory with the full support from the public and Congress; Michael Walzer, "The Argument about Humanitarian Intervention," Dissent 49, no. 1 (Winter 2002): 29-37. Waltzer states that we are more intimately engaged in intervention than we were in the past. He questions whether it is the United States' responsibility to intervene, and what might be moral justifications for such interventions.

intervention.[4] In order to accomplish these various tasks, the U.S. military serves as the action arm for the nation by reacting to policymaker decisions and their ability to either fund or direct these requirements. Often this funding and direction, coupled with the compassion of the nation, has led to United States intervention in the form of military operations other than war (OOTW).[5] The United States assistance to humanitarian relief operations has also required such military support.[6] It was this understanding in December 1992, and September 1994 that led the U.S. military to intervene in both Africa and the Caribbean, respectively.

In both situations, starvation in the Africa country of Somalia and the Caribbean country of Haiti was epidemic. In Somalia, the dire humanitarian and security conditions affected hundreds of thousands of Somalis. These desperate individuals were on the verge of death as they left Somalia for the neighboring countries of Ethiopia and Kenya. The United Nations (UN) identified that Somalia lacked the capability to ensure security and stability over its sovereign territory prompting the international community to seek external assistance. In 1992, the U.S.

---

[4]Michael Walzer, *Just and Unjust Wars: A Moral Argument with Historical Illustrations*, 4th ed. (New York: Basic Books, 2006), 86.

[5]U.S. Department of Defense, Joint Publication 3-07: *Joint Doctrine for Military Operations Other Than War,* 1995 (Washington D.C.: The Joint Staff 1995), iv. *Operations other than war* is a historical U.S. joint military term that describes a diverse collection of military activities. The term includes the following activities: arms control, combating terrorism, counter drug operations, sanctions/maritime intercept operations, enforcing exclusion zones, and freedom of navigation and over flight, humanitarian assistance, military support to civil authorities, nation assistance/support to counterinsurgency, noncombatant evacuation, peace operations, strikes, raids, and support to insurgency.; U.S. Department of Defense, Joint Publication 3-07: *Stability Operations,* 2011 (Washington D.C.: The Joint Staff 2011), viii, xx, III-18, III-27, E-7. The current Joint Publication 3-07 removed *OOTW* from its lexicon, however the military activities are now referred to as *stability operations*. Stability operations encompass many missions where environments are more complex than they may at first appear.; U.S. Department of Defense, Joint Publication 3-07.3: *Peace Operations,* 2007 (Washington D.C.: The Joint Staff 2007); Margaret S. Salter, "Training for Operations Other Than War (Stability Operations): Front End Analysis," www.dtic.mil/cgi-bin/GetTRDoc?AD=ADA323247 (accessed July 31, 2012).

[6]Richard W. Stewart, *The United States Army in Somalia, 1992-1994* (Washington D.C.: U.S. Army Center of Military History: U.S. Government Publishing Office, 2002), 5.

Government answered the UN call contributing immensely to the overarching food and medical assistance mission.[7] Shortly after in 1994, over sixty thousand Haitians attempted to flee their country for the United States using various unsafe waterborne crafts. Unlike Somalia, however, this dire situation emerged after the international community initially imposed economic sanctions on the unstable Haitian Government in an effort to increase political pressure to restore democratic institutions to the second Republic in the Americas. Accordingly, these volatile security situations in Somalia and Haiti, coupled with struggles for humanitarian relief, eventually paved the way for United States interventions.

Purpose, Hypothesis, and Significance

The purpose of this research is to help leaders understand the nature of collaborative teams in complex humanitarian relief operations. To accomplish this, research will examine the U.S. Government efforts in Somalia from December 1992 to October 1993 and Haiti from September 1994 to March 1995. This study will also provide an understanding of how the employment of Special Operations Forces (SOF) and interagency organizations effectively support humanitarian relief operations.[8] This research, more importantly, also assumes that humanitarian relief operations in Somalia and Haiti will be necessary in the future given the long history of United States in OOTW.[9] Hence, popular support from the United States and the international community, in regards to funding and direction from the U.S. Government lends itself to the premise of this research. For this reason, any future United States led humanitarian

---

[7]George C. Herring, *From Colony to Superpower: U.S. Foreign Relations Since 1776* (New York: Oxford University Press, 2011), 925.

[8]The remainder of this research will term *departments*, *agencies*, and *organizations* as "organizations."

[9]Daniel P. Bolger, *Savage Peace: Americans at War in the 1990s* (California: Presidio, 1995), 267.

3

effort, or special operations intervention will require an evolution in interagency collaboration as a means to counter possible irregular threats.

The idea of interagency collaboration is not new. In fact, we can trace this collaboration back to 1846 and the United States' first foreign war. It was in Mexico where General Winfield Scott and Nicholas Trist set aside their differences to achieve the U.S. Government's political objectives.[10] As the literature review will discuss in the next section, the history of interagency collaboration uncovers several issues written about by a broad range of scholars. Collectively, these scholars from both academia and government circles have yet to discuss the relationship of interagency collaboration between "operational" military units like SOF, and "civilian" interagency organizations. This research in turn will contribute to the development of the study of interagency collaboration by positing effective recommendations for closing this gap.

The significance of this study is based on its implications for the strategic, operational, and tactical levels of war. For instance, at the strategic level, this study captures several considerations for military and civilian leaders before deciding to engage in humanitarian relief operations. Given that no operation rests solely in the scope of any one department or agency, current and future military operations in Somalia and Haiti will require the military to work with interagency organizations. Indeed, the number of organizations that share primary responsibilities in providing relief often adds to the complexity of humanitarian relief operations. Furthermore, this interdependency has led to the development of a new United States Geographical Combatant Command – U.S. Africa Command (USAFRICOM) – where civilian leadership is integrated throughout all levels of the decision making process. However, planning for such integration at USAFRICOM did not account for the varied organizational cultures that exist, or seek to exist,

---

[10]Timothy D. Johnson, *A Gallant Little Army: The Mexico City Campaign* (Kansas: The University of Kansas, 2007), 113, 267. During the Mexican-American War, U.S. Army Commanding General Winfield Scott, and political appointee, Nicholas Trist met the political objective—American expansionism.

within the command.[11] For instance, at the operational level, this study uncovers an understanding of prior issues with the execution of humanitarian relief operations in both Somalia and Haiti. While no operation is the same, history highlights causative factors leading to success, as well as missteps, in prior operations. In order to prepare for this future, branches, and sequels to joint, interagency, and multinational plans and planning are required. At the tactical level, this study informs military and civilian operators of the aforementioned considerations so that tactical level planning can integrate with larger military operations. Additionally, understanding the informal and actual political power structure, as well as the dynamics between the two, is important throughout the spectrum highlighted above.[12] The implications of this research are vast. However, the literature review will address three areas of collaboration that attempt to narrow this study so that leaders can ensure the safety of human lives when deciding whether to support future intervention.

LITERATURE REVIEW

The previous section introduced the topic of U.S. military engagements in OOTW, specifically focusing on humanitarian relief operations in Somalia from December 1992 to October 1993 and in Haiti from September 1994 to March 1995. That section also introduced the purpose of the study, stated the hypothesis, and provided the study's significance. This section, in turn, uncovers perspectives on interagency and SOF collaboration in three areas. The first area examines what some have called "a hamstrung and broken" system.[13] In recent years, authors

---

[11]Kimberly Nastasi Klein, *Establishing U.S. Africa Command,* Washington D.C.: Project on National Security Reform http://old.pnsr.org/web/page/932/sectionid/579/pagelevel/3/parentid/590/interior.asp (accessed February 3, 2013).

[12]John P. Abizaid and John R, Wood, "Preparing for Peacekeeping: Military Training and the Peacekeeping Environment," *Special Warfare* 7, no. 2 (April 1994): 14-20.

[13]Geoffrey C. Davis and John F. Tierney, "The Need for Interagency Reform:

have increasingly published journal and magazine articles requesting interagency reform. This area will answer two questions, what is the interagency, and why is it hamstrung and broken? The second area examines the elite and highly trained operatives of SOF. This area will answer two questions about SOF; who are they, and what is so special about them? The third area will explore three weaknesses minimizing the efficiency and effectiveness of national security organizations.

What is the Interagency?

Congressmen Geoffrey Davis and John Tierney have stated that while the idea of interagency organizations is plausible, the policymaking process is "hamstrung and broken."[14] Accordingly, strategic leaders and policymakers of the three branches of the U.S. Government provide broad guidance and funding to civilian and military organizations. The reliance of interpreting this broad guidance frequently requires discourse with more than one organization. Congressman Davis defined *interagency operations* as, "Operations conducted by two or more federal departments or agencies in support of a national security mission."[15] While this articulation is appropriate, the interagency is much broader than this definition alone. This research, for this reason, defines *interagency* as a collaborative forum where complex organizations, each having different roles, responsibilities, and cultures, from government organizations meet to discuss implementation of a variety of specific strategic goals and objectives. Given that U.S. Government strategy, stratements to Congress, and briefings to the

---

Congressional Perspective and Efforts," *InterAgency Journal* 3, no. 1 (Winter 2012): 3. Congressman Davis was a Republican from Kentucky and Congressman Tierney was a Democrat from Massachusetts.

[14]Davis and Tierney, "The Need for Interagency Reform: Congressional Perspective and Efforts," 3.

[15]Geoffrey Davis, "Interagency Reform: The Congressional Perspective," *Military Review* 88, no. 4 (July-August 2008): 2.

media identify the goals and objectives of strategic leaders, the *interagency process* in turn, is where the strategic goals are interprented, integrated (or synchronized), and tasked to departments and agencies for implementation.[16] As federal budget deficits continue to constrain department and agency equities, this process leands itself to a highly confrontational and likely intensely political discourse regarding funding, roles, and organizational responsibilities.

The framework for interagency forums began nearly sixty years ago, following World War II, when President Truman sent a message to Congress recommending reform.[17] This concept was initially enacted through the 1947 National Security Act (NSA-1947), which created a cabinet-level civilian Department of Defense (DoD) Secretary to direct the execution of the separate departments – Army, Navy, and Air Force.[18] As action arms for national interests, these branches received a secretary to better integrate planning for military services. Additionally, the NSA-1947 established the wartime Joint Chiefs of Staff, which included a Chairman to serve dually as the senior military advisor to the President and the Secretary of Defense. Since 1947, the United States has been challenged by global interdependence, weakened Cold War alliances, sub-state and non-state actors, and increased international resistance to diplomatic pressure. More importantly, new chemical, biological, and cyber threats have evolved to a level that significantly

---

[16]U.S. Department of Defense, Joint Publication 3-0: *Joint Operations,* 2011 (Washington D.C.: Headquarters, The Joint Chiefs of Staff 2011). U.S. Government strategy documents such as the National Security Strategy, the National Defense Strategy, the National Military Strategy, regional strategies designated by the Department of State, the National Counterterrorism Strategy, or any other strategic guidance issued by senior U.S. policymakers, provides the context for strategic goals and aims of the U.S. Government.

[17]John F. Tierney, House Committee on Oversight and Government Reform: Subcommittee on National Security and Foreign Affairs, *National Security, Interagency Collaboration, and Lessons from SOUTHCOM and AFRICOM,* 111th Congress, 2nd Session, 2010, 1.

[18]Ibid.

threaten United States infrastructure.[19] According to *Forging a New Shield*, "the U.S. national security system is still organized to win the last challenge, not the ones that come increasingly before us." Given these threats, as well as austere federal budgets, the state of the world necessitates interagency approaches to meet and deter these national challenges.

The NSA-1947, however, did not solely modify the DoD; this act also put forth modifications to government business more broadly. For instance, the expanded role of the President of the United States necessitated a staff to assist him. This staff, more commonly known as the National Security Staff (NSS), received a mandate, but not the authority, to better coordinate policy on behalf of the President.[20] Before 1947, the coordination for foreign policies and a national security agenda rested solely on the shoulders of the President.[21]

Today, the President of the United States shares responsibility for the interagency process with Congressional leaders. Congressmen Davis and Tierney's article describes the modern challenges of interagency collaboration, and further identifies that Congress shares part-ownership of the impediments to the interagency process.[22] Although not integrated into the interagency process, these congressmen believe that organizations such as the Departments of Agriculture, Justice, and Treasury are crucial components to national security. Congressmen

---

[19]James R. Clapper, "Unclassified Statement for the Record On the Worldwide Threats Assessment of the U.S. Intelligence Community for the Senate Select Committee On Intelligence" (Washington D.C.: Office of the Director of National Intelligence, 2012), www.intelligence.senate.gov/120131/clapper.pdf (accessed December 12, 2012).

[20]Herring, *From Colony to Superpower*, 614. NSA-1947 also created an independent Central Intelligence Agency to replace the Office of Strategic Services.

[21]Office of the Historian, "National Security Act of 1947," U.S. Department of State http://history.state.gov/milestones/1945-1952/NationalSecurityAct (accessed September 27, 2012). The NSS is the President of the United States' principal staff to assist in coordinating and assessing implementation of strategic decisions. The NSC is the President's principal forum for considering national security and foreign policy matters with the senior national security advisors, as well as senior officials from throughout the interagency.

[22]Ibid.

Davis and Tierney also stated that, "there are regulatory, budgetary, legislative, bureaucratic, and cultural impediments to effective interagency operations."[23] These leaders articulated that the variety of the threats we face requires that the aforementioned organizations be resourced and staffed with interagency operations in mind.[24] While this broad guidance is essential, the research of analysis in the subsequent case studies (The Battle for Mogadishu in 1992-93 and The Battle for Haiti 1994-95) finds that understanding among interagency, and competition among intra-organizations, impacted U.S. Government progress against these two national challenges.

Why is the interagency a hamstrung and broken system?

While there are numerous variables influencing the effectiveness of national security organizations, this monograph sides with *Forging a New Shield,* in that "the system," not one individual organization, is "imbalanced" and requires an evolution.[25] The function of the NSC is to "advise the President with respect to the integration of domestic, foreign, and military policies relating to the national security so as to enable the military services and the other [organizations] of the [U.S.] Government to cooperate more effectively in matters involving national security."[26] The NSC further seeks to protect and defend the United States from foreign and domestic security threats by integrating all elements of national power (diplomatic, informational, military, economic, law enforcement, and intelligence), but the NSC has historically been "vulnerable to

---

[23]Davis and Tierney, "The Need for Interagency Reform: Congressional Perspective and Efforts," 3.

[24]Davis, "Interagency Reform," 4.

[25]Project on National Security Reform, "Forging a New Shield" http://0183896.netsolhost.com/site/wp-content/uploads/2011/12/pnsr-forging_exec-summary_12-2-08.pdf (accessed March 10, 2013).

[26]U.S. Congress, "National Security Act of 1947 (Public law 253, 80th Congress, July 26, 1947, 61 Stat. 495) as amended to January 8, 1952, and including the National Security Act amendments of 1949, Public law 216, 81st Congress, August 10, 1949, 63 Stat. 578," ed. 80th Congress (Washington D.C.: U.S. Government Printing Office, 1952).

breakdown during periods of transition between administrations."[27] In subsequent ratifications to NSA-1947, however, the NSC did not receive the mandate to directly synchronize, with appropriate authority, the same instruments of national power as a means to pursue the president's strategic goals in whole or in part through the arrangement of actions in time, space, and purpose.[28] Former Secretary of Defense Clark Clifford and the late U.S. Diplomat Richard Holbrooke called the NSC a "government within a government, which could evade oversight of its activities by drawing a cloak of secrecy about itself."[29] Within any forum, the addition of new organizations brings more complexity to the process of collaboration. As the Project on National Security Reform suggests, "A burdened [NSC] cannot manage the national security system as a whole to be agile and collaborative at any time."[30] According to Clay Runzi, "bureaucratic leveraging, vacillating presidential prerogative, and unique signature threats of the 21st Century clearly demonstrate that the NSC not only falls short of the initial Congressional intent in 1947, but [they] also [fall short] on the reality of [today's] requirements."[31] In the same year, Bob Ulin

---

[27]Project on National Security Reform, "Forging a New Shield" http://0183896.netsolhost.com/site/wp-content/uploads/2011/12/pnsr-forging_exec-summary_12-2-08.pdf (accessed March 10, 2013); White House, "Fact Sheet: Procedures Implementing Section 1022 of the National Defense Authorization Act for Fiscal Year 2012," http://www.whitehouse.gov/sites/default/files/ndaa_fact_sheet.pdf (accessed March 13, 2012). According to this White House publication, the elements of national power also includes law enforcement and intelligence.

[28]The theory of modern operational art describes the synchronization (implies authority) of the necessary instruments of national power in pursuit of strategic objectives in whole or in part, through the arrangement of actions in time and space for a specific purpose. This idea is not limited to one specific level of war.

[29]Herring, *From Colony to Superpower*, 614.

[30]Project on National Security Reform, "Forging a New Shield" http://0183896.netsolhost.com/site/wp-content/uploads/2011/12/pnsr-forging_exec-summary_12-2-08.pdf (accessed March 10, 2013).

[31]Clay O. Runzi, "Transforming the National Security Council: Interagency Authority, Organization, Doctrine." (MSSD Monograph, U.S. Army War College, 2007), 1.

emphasizes that, "a major problem in the operation of the U.S. Government is the difficulty, if not the inability, to delegate authority below the President level across department and agency borders."[32] This bottleneck prevents the NSC system from linking the skills and expertise necessary to solve complex and ambiguous problems from within the government.[33] As we will find in the third area of the literature review, this control over government further limits the efficiency and effectiveness of planning and ideas.

On July 31, 2012, the leading voice in Congress for interagency collaboration resigned.[34] It is likely that Congressman Davis' departure from Congress will not only delay congressional discourse on interagency reform, but it will also delay congressional decision on bill proposals introducing such reform.[35] The United States deserves a cohesive and effective body that produces coordinated, continuous planning, and timely actions that drive whole-of-government approaches to complex and ambiguous issues. This approach assumes that relevant entities from within government will want to contribute in assigned roles and functions to achieve strategic interests. This necessity for a strategy-centric planning process also implies a requirement for continuous assessments to ensure plans, planning, and actions, remain aligned to the strategic intent.[36] This planning process would likely achieve success if implemented at more junior-levels

---

[32]Bob Ulin, "About Interagency Cooperation," *InterAgency Essay* no. 10-01, (2010): 2.

[33]Project on National Security Reform, "Forging a New Shield" http://0183896.netsolhost.com/site/wp-content/uploads/2011/12/pnsr-forging_exec-summary_12-2-08.pdf (accessed March 10, 2013).

[34]U.S. Congress, House., *Offices of the Fourth Congressional District of Kentucky to Remain Open to Serve and Assist Constituents*, by Office of the Clerk of the House of Representatives http://clerk.house.gov/about/press/08012012_01.aspx (accessed February 3, 2013).

[35]U.S. Congress. Senate., *Interagency Personnel Rotation Act of 2011,* Senate of the United States (Washington D.C.: Congressional Record, 2011). http://www.govtrack.us/congress/bills/112/s1268 (accessed November 2, 2012).

[36]At more operational levels, joint interagency coordination groups, joint interagency task

given that, "informal relationships are at least as important as the formal machinery, and are critical to each agency understanding the business and equalities of the other agencies."[37] Within the DoD, the business of SOF is often mysteriously and frequently over exaggerated. The lack of sufficient understanding on whom SOF are hampers not only interagency operations but also intra-organization professional development and understanding. The second area of the literature review seeks to chip away at the mysteriousness of SOF. To accomplish this, we ask who is SOF, and what is so special about them?

Who are Special Operations Forces?

Andrew Feickert, a retired Army Special Forces officer, says that, "[SOF] are elite military units with special training and equipment that *can* infiltrate hostile territory through land, sea, or air to conduct a variety of operations, many of them classified."[38] It is no secret that the "physical and political risk, operational techniques, mode of employment, and dependence on detailed operational intelligence and indigenous assets" sets SOF apart from conventional military forces.[39] James Kiras, a professor at the School of Advanced Air and Space Studies said, "because SOF are super-elite soldiers, and therefore very few in number, they can only be employed with surprise in brief bursts of action."[40] It is also no secret that SOF often operate

---

forces, terrorism exploitation financial units, and theater security cooperation working groups are often effective interagency forums.

[37]Paul R. Pillar, *Terrorism and U.S. Foreign Policy* (Washington D.C.: Brookings Institution Press, 2003), 124. Pillar is a nonresident senior fellow with Foreign Policy at Brookings Institution. He retired in 2005 after serving 25 years in the U.S. Government.

[38] Andrew Feickert, "U.S. Special Operations Forces (SOF) Background and Issues for Congress" (Washington D.C.: Congressional Research Service, 2012), 1.

[39]U.S. Department of Defense, Joint Publication 3-05: *Special Operations,* 2011 (Washington D.C.: Headquarters, The Joint Chiefs of Staff 2011), ix.

[40]James Kiras, *Special Operations and Strategy: From World War II to the War on Terrorism* (New York: Routledge, 2006), xi.

clandestinely; in denied and/or politically sensitive environments.[41] Many authors describe elements of "the dark" or "the black" side of military SOF, with coined terms such as *"Delta," "Rangers," "Green Berets," "SEALs,"* or *"160th SOAR,"* however, little attention is paid to the softer, more "vanilla" or "the white" side of their responsibility.[42] Title 10, Section 167, of U.S. Code provides and explains SOF core activities. These activities authorize SOF to conduct a variety of missions ranging from: "direct action, strategic reconnaissance, unconventional warfare, foreign internal defense, civil affairs (CA), military information support operations, counterterrorism, psychological operations (PSYOP), humanitarian assistance, theater search and rescue, and other activities specified by the President of the United States and the Secretary of Defense."[43] With these activities come specific tools, such as education and training, to assist in the implementation of the larger policy goals and objectives for partnered nations.

According to Kiras, "the primary utility of special operations [forces] is to improve performance by increasing the military effectiveness of friendly forces, accomplishing political

---

[41]U.S. Department of Defense, Joint Publication 3-05*: Special Operations,* 2011 (Washington D.C.: Headquarters, The Joint Chiefs of Staff, 2011), I-1.

[42]Mark Bowden, *Black Hawk Down: A Story of Modern War* (New York: Atlantic Monthly Press, 1999). Bowden referred to *D-boys* and *The Rangers* in his novel.; Robin Moore, *The Green Berets* (New York: Crown Publishers, 1965). Moore was known for his account of "The Green Berets," (subsequently a movie starring John Wayne during the start of the Tet-Offensive in South Vietnam).; Dick Couch, *The Warrior Elite: The Forging of Seal Class 228* (New York: Crown Publishers, 2001). Couch describes that it takes to become a U.S. Navy SEAL in his novel.; Michael J. Durant, Steven Hartov, and Robert L. Johnson, *The Night Stalkers: Top Secret Missions of the U.S. Army's Special Operations Aviation Regiment* (New York: G.P. Putnam's Sons, 2006). Durant describes what it was like to be shot down in his Blackhawk helicopter in Mogadishu during the Battle of Mogadishu.

[43]For a comprehensive list of SOF activities, see U.S. Special Operations Command, "About USSOCOM," USSOCOM, http://www.socom.mil/Pages/AboutUSSOCOM.aspx (accessed March 2, 2013); Government Printing Office, *United States Code, 2006 Edition, Supplement 5, Title 10 - Armed Forces,* 2012 (Washington D.C.: Congress, 111th 2012). http://www.gpo.gov/fdsys/search/pagedetails.action?packageId=USCODE-2011-title10&granuleId=USCODE-2011-title10-subtitleA-partI-chap6-sec167 (accessed November 12, 2012).

and military objectives in a timely, economic manner, but also upsetting the adversary's strategic and operational calculus."[44] While Kiras takes a different approach than most authors, he captures the more "vanilla," or the capacity building side of SOF. Given the nature of their training, SOF are effective contributors to bringing security and stability to international efforts.[45]

What is so special about Special Operations Forces?

The nature of SOF activities requires that they be highly proficient and experienced war fighters with advanced training and education. As of January 2012, the U.S. Special Operations Command (USSOCOM) consisted for approximately sixty-three thousand active duty, National Guard, and reserve component, SOF operators. As explained above, these operators are employed in the Navy as SEALs (Sea, Air, Land); in the Air Force as combat aircraft controllers, pararescuemen, special operations weathermen, and combat aviation advisors; in the Marine Corps as critical skills operators; and in the Army as CA, special operations aviators, sustainers, military information support operations, rangers, and special forces.[46] In addition to the stealthy tactical training that SOF operators receive, they also receive interagency training and education from USSOCOM. Joint Special Operations University's (JSOU) Interagency Education Program contributes to SOF's professional development by providing an understanding of the SOF and interagency communities. Among other things, this education includes a strategic dialogue on the authorities of each community.[47]

---

[44]Kiras, *Special Operations and Strategy*, 79.

[45]For a useful introduction to SOF, see David Tucker and Christopher J. Lamb, *United States Special Operations Forces* (New York: Columbia University Press, 2007).

[46]U.S. Special Operations Command, *U.S. Special Operations Command Fact Book 2013* (Tampa, Florida: Headquarters, 2012), 10, 48-51.

[47]For more on JSOU training, see U.S. Joint Special Operations University, "2011 JSOU Publications" https://jsou.socom.mil/Pages/2011JSOUPublications.aspx (accessed October 3, 2012).

Conventional military forces tend to be apprehensive when it comes to irregular warfare (IW), however SOF are more comfortable with this particular type of war.[48] In IW, the enemy tends to fight within crowds of civilians and populations of noncombatants. After failed attempts to defeat an elusive enemy, conventional military forces are likely to forget the type of war that they are fighting, and cause cascading damage to the overall efforts of United States intervention.[49] As Colin S. Gray points out, in their frustration, conventional forces are likely to "do what energetic, career-minded soldiers are suppose to do: take the offensive, try to seize the initiative, and display much activity."[50] However, Gray believes that this mindset in IW is not very helpful.[51] Regardless, simulating these environments may increase the comfort of militaries before operating in these crowded environments.[52] The third area of the literature review takes a

---

[48] IW is "a struggle among state and nonstate actors for legitimacy and influence over the relevant populations." U.S. Department of Defense, Joint Publication 1-02: *Department of Defense Dictonary of Military and Associated Terms* (Washington D.C.: Headquarters, The Joint Chiefs of Staff, 2010), 161; U.S. Department of Defense, "Irregular Warfare Joint Operating Concept Version 1.0" www.fas.org/irp/doddir/dod/iw-joc.pdf (accessed January 31, 2013). IW favors indirect and asymmetrical approaches, though it may employ the full-range of military and other capabilities to erode an adversary's power, influence, and will.; For a recent SAMS monograph that argues for a seventh warfighting function, see Jan Kenneth Gleiman, "Operational Art and the Clash of Organizational Cultures: Postmortem on Special Operations as a Seventh Warfighting Function," (MMAS Monograph, Command and General Staff College, 2011).

[49] Colin S. Gray, *War, Peace and International Relations: An Introduction to Strategic History* (New York: Routledge, 2007), 256. Colin S. Gray is a British-American scholar and professor of international relations and strategic studies at the University of Reading in England – he additionally is an external researcher for the U.S. Army War College.

[50] Gray, *War, Peace and International Relations: An Introduction to Strategic History*, 256.

[51] Ibid.

[52] In 1999, Bruce Stanley stated, "One way to overcome [the] problem of training and education in peacetime is through the use of computer wargames." Stanley suggests that wargames lead to professional development and decisiveness in time-constrained environments. Bruce E. Stanley, "Wargames, Training, and Decision-Making: Increasing the Experience of Army Leaders" (MMAS Monograph, Command and General Staff College, 1999).

synthesis of both SOF and interagency efforts to examine the efficiency and effectiveness of national security organizations.

Efficiency and Effectiveness of National Security Organizations

Contemporary literature on national security finds three weaknesses affecting the efficiency and effectiveness of national security organizations. These weaknesses include the lack of interagency training and education, the lack of a unified strategic vision for interagency cooperation; and the lack of organizational-level commitment to whole-of-government approaches. These three weaknesses, if properly advocated, appropriately funded, and successfully implemented across government, could streamline national level collaboration on U.S. Government challenges by unifying stove piped efforts and mandating collaboration with other governmental organizations. This idea focuses on the human element of information sharing verses the technological aspect of information sharing.

Interagency Training and Education

The first obstacle affecting the efficiency and effectiveness of interagency collaboration on matters of national level challenges involves interagency training and education.[53] Even though strategic documents may espose collaborative efforts across government, interagency coordination is not perfect; there are challenges such as training an education that senior leaders can fix.[54] "Some U.S. Government [organizations] lack the personnel capacity to fully participate

---

[53] U.S. Government Accountability Office, "An Overview of Professional Development Activities Intended to Improve Interagency Collaboration," http://www.gao.gov/assets/320/312349.pdf (accessed November 17, 2012). The GAO identified 225 professional developmental activities intended to improve participants' ability to collaborate across agency/department boundaries.; John E. O'Neil IV, "The Interagency Process – Analysis and Reform Recommendations" (U.S. Army War College, 2006), 10.

[54]Pillar, *Terrorism and U.S. Foreign Policy*, 125.

in interagency activities."[55] Allowing an individual to attend training would potentially leave a hole in the production of the parent organization.[56] Creating opportunities for interagency training and education would require a congressional mandate to ensure implementation broadly across the U.S. Government.

Despite the lack of more formalized congressional oversight to interagency training and education programs, leaders continue to provide opportunities to develop the next generation of leaders.[57] Organizations such as the Departments of Defense, State, and Homeland Security, provide the bulk of training and education opportunities for non-military employees within the U.S. Government.[58] Additionally, USSOCOM provides training courses several times a year to prepare military and civilian leaders to collaborate successfully within interagency communities.[59] Furthermore, senior military schools such as the Command and General Staff College (CGSC), the Army, Air, Naval, and Marine War Colleges, the National Defense University, Joint Forces Staff College, as well as the intelligence community and federal law

---

[55]U.S. Government Accountability Office, "Key Issues for Congressional Oversight of National Security Strategies, Organizations, Workforce, and Information Sharing," http://www.gao.gov/assets/210/203867.pdf (accessed November 17, 2012).

[56]Ibid.

[57]Assessments on the program and its effectiveness would hold organizations responsible for the lack of efficiency and effectiveness.

[58]U.S. Government Accountability Office, "An Overview of Professional Development Activities Intended to Improve Interagency Collaboration," http://www.gao.gov/assets/320/312349.pdf (accessed November 17, 2012). In 2010, GAO specified the DoD, DoS, and Department of Homeland Security providing the most professional developmental activities across the U.S. Government.

[59]Charles Ricks, *Special Operations Forces Interagency Counterterrorism Reference Manual*, 2nd ed. (Tampa, Florida: Joint Special Operations University, 2011). Located in Tampa, Florida, the USSOCOM created the Joint Special Operations University to educate SOF, as well as executives, senior and intermediate leaders, and select national and international security decision-makers, both from within the military and civilian cultures. The Joint Special Operations University educates through teaching, outreach, and research in the science and art of joint special operations.

enforcement schools, all seek more joint and interagency collaboration.[60] Through the

Department of State (DoS) programs, these schools have welcomed multinational participation

within the United States. Mathew Wilder, a former interagency student at CGSC, believed that

training outside ones' own organization could provide an increased level of understanding about

the capabilities and capacities of other organizations.[61]

Located at Fort Leavenworth, Kansas, CGSC has sought to attract interagency

representation in recent years to attend not only CGSC but also programs offered by the School of

Advanced Military Studies (SAMS) in their second and third years at Fort Leavenworth.[62]

Students from homeland security organizations (i.e. Departments of: Defense Justice, State,

Veterans Affairs; and Agencies such as: the Defense Intelligence Agency and the National

Geospatial Agency), join mid-level or senior-level military officers in a 9-12 month program.[63]

The two programs at SAMS focus on developing an appreciation for military leadership,

logistics, history, theory, doctrine national security policy, strategy, operations, and military plans

and planning, in order to anticipate and articulate recommendations for future problems.[64]

---

[60]Ulin, "About Interagency Cooperation," 5.

[61]Mathew Wilder, "Achieving Unity of Effort," *InterAgency Journal* 3, no. 1 (Winter 2011): 42.

[62]As part of CGSC, SAMS includes two programs, the Advanced Military Studies Program (second year) and the Advanced Operational Art Studies Fellowship (third year) provide a unique opportunity for interagency students, at the graduate-level, "to be agile and adaptive leaders who think critically at the strategic and operational levels to solve complex and ambiguous problems." School of Advanced Military Studies, "School of Advanced Military Studies: Trifold," SAMS http://usacac.army.mil/cac2/cgsc/Events/SAMS25th/SAMSTri-fold.pdf (accessed December 3, 2012).

[63]Ibid.; Kevin Benson, "School of Advanced Military Studies: Commemorative History 1984-2009," Command and General Staff College http://usacac.army.mil/cac2/cgsc/Events/SAMS25th/SAMS25YearsHistory.pdf (accessed February 3, 2013), 51-54.

[64]Benson, "School of Advanced Military Studies: Commemorative History 1984-2009," Command and General Staff College

Students are able to earn a Masters degree in Military Art and Science (MMAS), given CGSC's accreditation from the North Central Association of Colleges and Schools.[65] These training programs contributes to the overall professionalism of the U.S. Government Wilder believed, and this author can affirm, "[t]hese educational opportunities provide insights regarding the roles, authorities, and capabilities of other organizations that are difficult to obtain while in one's own comfort zone."[66]

Unified Strategic Vision for Interagency Cooperation

The second obstacle affecting the efficiency and effectiveness of national security organizations involves a lack of a unified strategic vision for interagency cooperation. A unified strategic vision could create standards for collaboration, and might serve as a way of holding organizations accountable for achieving unity-of-effort throughout government. Without this unified strategic vision, the government does not provide a coherent, cost-effective, and complementing solution to national security organization collaboration.

Congressional progress, although stalled since October 2011, appears to have taken the initial steps toward interagency reform.[67] If enacted into public law, an *Interagency Personnel Rotation Act* would establish a framework for training and education programs. The proposed 2011 bill had three primary objectives that advocated for collaboration and professional

---

http://usacac.army.mil/cac2/cgsc/Events/SAMS25th/SAMS25YearsHistory.pdf (accessed February 3, 2013), 51-54.

[65]North Central Association of Colleges and Schools, "Higher Learning Commission: U.S. Army Command and General Staff College," The Higher Learning Commission http://www.ncahlc.org/component/com_directory/Action,ShowBasic/Itemid,/instid,2036/ (accessed December 6, 2012).

[66]Wilder, "Achieving Unity of Effort," 42.

[67]U.S. Congress. Senate, "Interagency Personnel Rotation Act of 2011." Senate of the United States (Washington D.C.: Congressional Record, 2011), 3.

development of interagency personnel whose "primary duties relate to national security or homeland security policy formulation or execution."[68] The first objective was to create a U.S. Government employee rotational program for employees with roles in national security. The second objective required these employees to participate in training and education to further breakdown organizational cultural biases. The third objective would provide incentives to competent national security personnel who participated in interagency training and education environments.[69] The creation and enactment of such a bill by Congress and the President, followed by implemented across national security organizations, would greatly impact the efficiency and effectiveness of national security organizations.

Since the end of World War II, American officials have raised the issue of developing an interagency cadre development program. Advocates stated that the creation of such a program would enable interagency collaboration at and below the strategic level of government. Following the terrorist attacks on September 11, 2001, there has been an increased sense of urgency in such dialogue. Since this time, it has generally been understood that whole-of-government approaches to complex problems are essential for national security. However, as the two case studies below illuminate, this concept has not become second nature among national security organizations.

Organizational-Level Commitment to Whole-of-Government

The third obstacle affecting the efficiency and effectiveness of national security organizations involves organizational-level commitment (from senior leadership) to whole-of-government approaches to solving complex and ambiguous problems. Often organizations interpret strategic guidance as complicated, complex, and ambiguous. To avoid this unnecessary confusion, organizational leaders must provide clear and unambiguous guidance to their

---

[68]Ibid.

[69]Davis, "Interagency Reform," 6.

workforce to reduce the levels of complexness. To improve individual interagency collaboration, organizations might consider incentivizing opportunities for collaboration. Steward Patrick and Kaysie Brown, of the Center for Global Development, advocate that senior officials "create professional incentives to reward greater interagency collaboration."[70]

Incentives might directly link into the individual annual performance evaluations. The narrative leaders use to communicate the seriousness of these efforts would likely produce organizational-level support for collaboration. Patrick and Brown also discuss, the possibility of linking professional advancement to "joint" or "interagency service" as a possible way of overcoming a resistance from employees. Collaboration could be linked to professional advancement to "joint" or "interagency service," for example, a DoD employee (civilian or military), with appropriate planning experience, might be rewarded by selection to participate in an interagency opportunity. This idea of joint-duty or exchange programs, where two employees from different organizations switch to the others' organization, is an effective means to cross coordinate informally before formal organizational permissions are granted.[71] Military and civilian joint-duty, or exchange programs, enables on-the-job training that enables competent participants to obtain first-hand awareness of institutional cultures, key decision maker interests, and the daily operations of a different organization. These programs are valuable not only to the individual participants, but also for the organizations involved in the program.

---

[70]Stewart Patrick and Kaysie Brown, *Greater Than the Sum of Its Parts? Assessing "Whole of Government" approaches to Fragile States* (Washington D.C.: International Peace Academy, 2007), 3.

[71]Thomas Countryman, "National Security, Interagency Collaboration, and Lessons from SOUTHCOM and AFRICOM," in *The Subcommittee on National Security and Foreign Affairs House Committee Oversight and Government Reform* (Washington D.C.: U.S. Department of State, 2010). http://democrats.oversight.house.gov/images/stories/subcommittees/NS_Subcommittee/7.28.10_Interagency_Africom_and_southcom/Countryman_Statement.pdf (accessed July 28, 2012).

The DoS provides an excellent model for joint-duty programs. For half a century, DoS has provided foreign political advisors, commonly referred to as "POLADs," to major military headquarters, combatant commands, and military units assigned within key conflict areas.[72] POLADs are not a shortened substitute for interagency coordination, however, they do serve as a means for senior military officers to facilitate coordination and improve policy development with the headquarters.[73] This process also provides a way to de-conflict policy issues early in the process through interagency collaboration. Coupled with policy de-confliction, having relevant organizations participating in the planning process allows planners to anticipate and address organizational differences in anticipated end states, objectives, and terms.[74] According to Thomas Countryman, DoS has established, "planning relationships with combatant commands, such as USAFRICOM [and United States Southern Command], to ensure whole-of-government planning efforts."[75] One underlining utility of interagency forums is that they offer an opportunity to really think conceptually and iteratively about whatever problem, or question, initiated the discourse. For instance, as U.S. military forces begin to draw down conventional forces from Afghanistan, conceptual planning would paint a picture for the detailed solution. Conceptual planning would seek a broad approach to remove conventional forces from Afghanistan given the constraints of time. Detailed planning would account for movement rates, shipping requirements, loading and unloading of gear, weapons, ammunition, etc. Depending on one's education, training, and

---

[72]Patrick and Brown, *Greater Than the Sum of Its Parts? Assessing "Whole of Government" approaches to Fragile States* (Washington D.C.: International Peace Academy, 2007), 3.

[73]Countryman, "National Security, Interagency Collaboration, and Lessons from SOUTHCOM and AFRICOM" (Washington D.C.: U.S. Department of State, 2010).

[74]Ibid.

[75]Bureau of Political-Military Affairs, "Office of the Coordinator of the Foreign Policy Advisor Program (PM/POLAD)," U.S. Department of State, http://www.state.gov/t/pm/polad/ (accessed September 27, 2012).

professional development, individuals identify different ways of leaving the discourse and

providing a fully functioning set of options for strategic leaders.

Table 1. Recommendations to Increase the Efficiency and Effectiveness of National Security Organizations

	Recommendation	Reasoning
1	Interagency Training and Education	Collaborative approaches to national security requires a well-trained workforce with the skills and experitise to integrate the government's diverse capabilities and resources.
2	Unified Strategic Vision for Interagency Cooperation	Organizations, if funded, need to be held accountable for achieving unity-of-effort for priority efforts of the government, without this the government fials to provide a coherent, cost-effective, complimenting solution to interagency problems.
3	Organizational-level Commitment to Whole-of-Government Approaches	Organizational leaders must provide unambiguous guidance to their workforce to improve individual interagency cooperation

Source: Created by author.

Summary

The literature review was broken down into three areas. The first introduced the

interagency and examined recent literature calling it "a hamstrung and broken system." The

second area introduced SOF and identified the SOF core activities. The third area reviewed

literature discussing the efficiency and effectiveness of national security organizations. Given this

understanding of the interagency and SOF, the research found three weaknesses minimizing the

efficiency and effectiveness of national security organizations. These three weaknesses provide

insight into opportunities for reform within in the U.S. Government's policymaking process. The

next section will discuss the methodology used to focus the remainder of this study. Following

the methodology, case studies on Somalia and Haiti begin with brief histories.

METHODOLOGY

This study will apply Alexander George's case study methodology to present a

comprehensive analysis of humanitarian relief operations in Somalia and Haiti from December

1992 to October 1993, and September 1994 to March 1995, respectively.[76] The assumption that the United States will be asked to return to support future UN humanitarian missions in Somalia and Haiti lends itself to a narration of this monograph's thesis. If the United States-led humanitarian efforts and special operations are required to counter irregular threats, then interagency communities will require an evolution in interagency collaboration. The two selected case studies explain how U.S. military forces in Somalia during Operation Restore Hope, and in Haiti during Operation Uphold Democracy, collectively encourage interagency reform.[77] Each case study will include a historical introduction, synopsis to understand the operational environment, a dialogue on major United States players, interagency and SOF actions, collaboration between the interagency and SOF, and the outcomes of United States intervention. Following the case studies, an overall synthesis of the research will highlight important similarities between the two studies. Following the synthesis, this monograph will conclude with observations and recommendations for the future of U.S. Government operations in order to increase the efficiency and effectiveness of national security organizations, specifically as they engage in humanitarian relief operations in the future.

The limitations in this study are many. Given language and classification restrictions, the analysis in this monograph only includes authorized information available within the public domain. While conducting research, economic and social issues were analyzed, but only to the extent that they affect the stability and security within Somalia and Haiti. Additionally, this study diverts focus from piracy and counter piracy operations. The next section will introduce Somalia and highlight important aspects for both case studies. The study of Somalia (1992-1993) and

---

[76]Alexander L. George and Andrew Bennett, *Case Studies and Theory Development in the Social Sciences* (Cambridge, MA.: The MIT Press, 2005).

[77]U.S. Government Accountability Office, "Improving Planning, Training, and Interagency Coordination Could Strengthen DOD's Efforts in Africa," http://www.gao.gov/assets/310/307759.pdf (accessed October 2, 2012).

Haiti (1994-1995), illustrates the assumption that the United States national security organizations as a whole requires reform. In context, each study compliments the other in form, style, and approach, lending room for a balanced conclusion and recommendations for future interagency and SOF collaboration.

CASE STUDIES

Somalia (1992-1993)

Introduction to Somalia

This section introduces the geography, her societal construct, as well as military and political issues leading to United States intervention in 1992. Before developing the operational environment, this section seeks to understand the divergent factors that contributed to some of the issues in Somalia. *Greater Somalia* includes nearly 242,216 square miles of territory; nearly the size of Texas.[78] Somalia borders the Gulf of Aden to the north, the Indian Ocean to the east, Kenya to the south, and Ethiopia and Djibouti to the west. In 1991, the people of Somaliland, the northwestern region of Somalia, declared themselves an independent state.[79] The self-proclaimed state of the Republic of Somaliland extends four hundred miles east of Djibouti and ebbs and flows into the Gulf of Aden to the north.[80] Since 1998, the self-declared Puntland region, the northeast region of Somalia, has been a self-governing and semi-autonomous state. Neighboring a

---

[78]*Greater Somalia* refers to the three contested regions of Somalia (Somalia, Puntland, and Somaliland), this paper will refer to these regions as *Somalia* unless otherwise described; Gray, *War, Peace and International Relations*, 226.

[79]Susan M. Hassig and Zawiah Abdul Latif, *Somalia* (New York: Marshall Cavendish Benchmark, 2008), 10.; Somaliland has not received international recognition from the African Union as an independent state. On January 17, 2008, the U.S. Government issued a statement of support to Somaliland as a regional administration for support programs, but that they would not recognize the region as an independent state.

[80]Ibid.

vital sea route linking the Indian Ocean to the Red Sea, Somalia is located in a region of strategic importance.[81] Figure 1 provides a basic map of the three regions of Somalia.[82]

Somalia has a common language and a common culture based on pastoral customs, religion, and traditions. The people of Somalia are largely pastoral nomads, who are well adapted to surviving in the harsh, arid terrain of the Horn of Africa, and share an abiding love for camels and poetry.[83] Generally, pastoral populations are very difficult to organize politically, and this is no different in Somalia.[84] Additionally, Somalis have shared a profound attachment to Islam. The practice of Islam in Somalia has been described as moderate, however, the conservative practice experienced in the Persian Gulf States is largely considered foreign to the Somali culture.[85] Somalis' oral traditions extend back to prehistory, tying them to the rules of antiquity and the family of Muhammad the Prophet.[86] Known for their lineage-based families, Somalis identify, in part, by their clan family.[87] The strongest basis for loyalty exists with immediate and extended

---

[81]Shaul Shay, *Somalia between Jihad and Restoration* (New Brunswick, N.J.: Transaction Publishers, 2010), vii.

[82]Hassig and Latif, *Somalia*, 10.

[83]Hassig and Latif, *Somalia*, 35.

[84]Martin Meredith, *The Fate of Africa: From the Hopes of Freedom to the Heart of Despair: A History of Fifty Years of Independence* (New York: Public Affairs, 2005), 464.

[85] Watts, Shapiro, and Brown make the point that nomads' mobility constrains any political movement seeking to establish a "secret base;" Somali nomads he says, "will contest any presence thy deem contrary to their interests." Clint Watts, Jacob Shapiro, and Vahid Brown, *Al-Qa'ida's (Mis)Adventures in the Horn of Africa* (West Point, New York: Combating Terrorism Center, 2007), 30.

[86] Ibid, 29.; *Prehistory* is a common term that refers to the time before written history.

[87]Bolger, *Savage Peace*, 267.

family. These same Somali families have historically also endured years of colonization, tyranny, civil war, and famine.[88]

Photo Removed Due to Copyright Restrictions

Figure 1: Somalia.

Source: "Somalia, Somaliland, and Puntland," Encyclopedia Britannica http://www.britannica.com/EBchecked/media/124811/The-Republic-of-Somalia-experienced-fragmentation-in-the-1990s-the (accessed February 13, 2013).

Understanding the Operational Environment

This section captured an understanding of the operational environment. The operational environment describes the circumstances affecting the situation as depicted in Somalia in 1992. In 1992, political instability reigned in Somalia. The dictatorship of Siad Barre, from 1969 to 1991, contributed to the rampant political instability and social oppression that has characterized Somalia for the past four decades. In the early 1990s, this instability saw three principal groups vying for power.[89] Those remaining in Somalia saw violent social factions held together by weak

---

[88]Scott Peterson, *Me Against My Brother: At War in Somalia, Sudan, and Rwanda: A Journalist Reports from the Battlefields of Africa* (New York: Routledge, 2000), 1.

[89]Cable News Network, "40 Killed as Troops Take Aim at Taliban," Cable News

political alliances, none of which were strong enough to unite and lead Somalia. Additionally, drought led to famine and collectively served as a spark to ignited ethnic tensions, which further increased this instability.[90] Table 2 provides a timetable of the three phases of operations in Somalia.

Table 2. Three Phases of United States Involvement in Somalia

Operation	Dates	U.N. Security Council Resolution
Provide Relief (UNOCOM I)	Aug. 15, 1992 – Dec. 9, 1992	UNSCR 751 (Apr. 24, 1992)
Restore Hope (UNITAF)	Dec. 9, 1992 – May 4, 1993	UNSCR 794 (Dec. 3, 1992)
UNOSOM II (USFORSOM)	May 4, 1993 – Mar. 31, 1994	UNSCR 814 (Mar. 26, 1993)

Source: Kenneth Allard, *Somalia Operations: Lessons Learned* (Washington D.C.: National Defense University Press, 1995), 12.

United Nations Security Council Resolution (UNSCR) 751, enacted April 24, 1992, made a politically volatile situation worse with the introduction of UN forces. This resolution opened the door to United Nations Operations in Somalia (UNOSOM) whose mission was to provide humanitarian aid and end hostilities in Somalia.[91] The deployed UN forces were not equipped to handle the massive security issues and widespread starvation facing the nation. Pursuant to UNSCR 751, UN Secretary-General Boutros-Ghali received a minimal commitment of fifty-unarmed observers, all of which came from Pakistan. This influx of fifty unarmed observers had

---

Network, http://articles.cnn.com/2006-06-15/world/fighting.taliban_1_operation-mountain-thrust-kandahar-and-zabol-provinces-coalition-forces?_s=PM:WORLD (accessed December 19, 2012). The three groups were the Somali National Movement (located in the north), the Somali Patriotic Movement (located in the South), the United Somali Congress (located near Mogadishu).

[90]Bolger, *Savage Peace*, 272.

[91]Bolger, *Savage Peace*, 274.

little effect.[92] By the summer of 1992, nearly three hundred thousand people had starved to death in Somalia.[93] As looting, gangs, and other lawlessness prevailed, aid did not reach those Somalis who needed it most.[94]

By mid-summer, the UN was accomplishing "next to nothing."[95] Given these security conditions, aid organizations could not distribute aid or provide much-needed relief services to the population.[96] In the countryside, gangs seized and amassed food stockpiles and used them as bargaining chips to project power over the local population. In the cities, the belligerent political factions, supported by their private armies, terrorized international organizations, stealing food and killing whoever did not pay protection money.[97] One account describes the violence in Mogadishu appropriately, "one day in late July, two UN relief flights to Mogadishu were halted on the runway and looted from nose to tail by clan gunmen, backed by their ever-present technical."[98] The technicals were pick up trucks with mounted machine guns used as a mobile weapon platform.[99] In Somalia, these weapons systems often consisted of a 50-caliber machine gun or similar machine guns mounted into the bed of imported vehicles. By mid-November, clans

---

[92]United Nations Security Council, "Resolution 751 (1992): as of 24 April 1992," United Nations (New York: UN Publications, 1992).

[93]Bolger, *Savage Peace*, 275.

[94]Ibid., 274.

[95]U.S. Department of the Army, *Field Manual 3-06, Appendix C: Operations in Somalia: Applying the Urban Operational Framework to Support and Stability,* 2006 (Washington D.C.: Headquarters, Department of the Army 2006).

[96]Ibid.

[97]Bolger, *Savage Peace*, 275.

[98]Stewart, *The United States Army in Somalia*, 8.

[99]Lauren Ploch, "Africa Command: U.S. Strategic Interests and the Role of the U.S. Military in Africa" (Washington D.C.: Congressional Research Service, 2011), 36-37.

armed with these improvised fighting vehicles effectively closed the Port of Mogadishu, further engulfing an already challenging situation.[100]

Clans, warlords, gangs, and armed militias stole whatever supplies the UN organizations were paying them to guard.[101] Dominant clan warlord, Mohamed Farrah Aideed and his fellow chieftains dominated the streets during the hours of aid delivery by ambushing UN aid vehicles transiting through their districts bound for rival-clan districts.[102] Only an estimated twenty-percent of the food entering the country was reaching the people who needed it.[103] Hijacking conveys, looting warehouses, and harassing relief workers, remained the plan of the day for warring factions, and they were effective at developing their personal stockpiles.[104]

Key Players

At the strategic level, key players in Somalia leading up to United States intervention in Somalia included the international television networks such as the Cable News Network (CNN), the U.S. President, DoS diplomats, and senior military decision-makers at the Pentagon. This was the first example of "the CNN effect," which has become an integral part of today's operational environment.[105] With the U.S. Presidential elections looming, Somalia was initially not a top

---

[100]Bolger, *Savage Peace*, 275.

[101]Ibid., 279.

[102]Ibid., 275, 279.; Aideed is frequently spelled "Aidid;" The American military would conclude that progress in Somalia could not be made until Aideed, the dominant clan warlord, and previous general in the Somali Army was neutralized.

[103]Gray, *War, Peace and International Relations*, 225.

[104]U.S. Department of the Army, *FM 3-06, Appendix C,* 2006 (Washington D.C.: Headquarters, Department of the Army, 2006).

[105]Kalb reports Somalia in 1992 as being the first example of "24-hour-a day, live television coverage broadcast from around the world." Marvin Kalb, "'The CNN Effect': How 24-Hour News Coverage Affects Government Decisions and Public Opinion," The Brookings Institution, http://www.brookings.edu/events/2002/01/23media-journalism (accessed January 31,

priority for the Bush Administration in early 1992, but the CNN effect would change this. Additionally, the UN played an important part throughout operations in Somalia, to include providing the mandate for contributing nations. However given their small contingent in Mogadishu, the UN sought assistance from the U.S. Government to shape and influence the deteriorating security conditions in Somalia. For the United States, understanding the capabilities of key international and intergovernmental players grew more important as operations advanced and key questions remained unanswered.

During this period, CNN broadcasted continuous footage of starving children who were covered with flies and living in filth. Hundreds of thousands, perhaps even millions of people, were at risk of starvation.[106] Madeleine Albright, then-the U.S. Ambassador to the UN, later stated that, "television's ability to bring graphic images of pain and outrage into our living rooms had heightened the pressure both for immediate engagement in areas of international crisis and immediate disengagement when events do not go according to plan."[107] For the U.S. President, "doing nothing" in Somalia would have been preferred, but the graphic images on television, coupled with the fact that President Herbert Walker Bush's democratic presidential opponent, William (Bill) Clinton, strongly supported the UN, led President Bush to react.[108] According to the *New York Times*, Bill Clinton "emphatically approved Mr. Bush's decision," in a written

---

2013).

[106]Bolger, *Savage Peace*, 279.

[107]John S. Brown, *Kevlar Legions: The Transformation of the U.S. Army, 1989-2005* (Washington D.C.: Center of Military History United States Army, 2011), 112.

[108]Madeleine K. Albright, "Building a Consensus on International Peace-keeping," *U.S. Department of State Dispatch*, October 20, 1993, 790. Following coalition victory during the Persian Gulf War the U.S. military was amid strategic downsizing, and ill-prepared for a humanitarian mission to Somalia.

statement, the *Times* reported Clinton as saying, "Impediments to delivery of relief supplies and particularly looting of life-saving food supplies simply must not be allowed to continue."[109]

In the fall of 1992, the UN requested an increased number of airlift supplies from the U.S. Government. President Bush was quick to respond by staging a small United States component in Kenya to deliver aid into remote areas of Somalia.[110] The Kenyans wanted to influence the planning and ideas of the U.S. Government, but the Kenyans reluctantly accepted the expanded U.S. military presence inside of Kenya.[111] Smith Hempstone, then-U.S. Ambassador to Kenya, and Marine Brigadier General Frank Libutti, Commander of the Joint Task Force, convinced the Kenyan Government that the United States presence would remain small in size, limited in its mission to flying aid into Somalia, and would withdraw completely once the tasks were complete.[112] These U.S. officials suggested that the tasks should be complete within a few months of operations.[113] Additionally, the U.S. officials informed the Kenyans that non-governmental organizations already in Somalia would distribute the aid and supplies.[114]

---

[109]Michael Wines, "Mission to Somalia; Bush Declared Goal in Somalia to 'save Thousands'," *New York Times*, December 5, 1992. http://www.nytimes.com/1992/12/05/world/mission-to-somalia-bush-declares-goal-in-somalia-to-save-thousands.html?src=pm (accessed January 31, 2013).

[110]"Unable to explain to the world why the "sole remaining superpower" and leader of the "new world order," was not able to stop the starvation, President Bush ordered U.S. forces to deploy to Somalia." Bolger, *Savage Peace*, 275; Thomas M. Montgomery, *United States Forces, Somalia After Action Report and Historical Overview: The United States Army in Somalia, 1992-1994* (Washington D.C.: Center of Military History, 2003).

[111]U.S. Department of the Army, *FM 3-06, Appendix C*, 2006 (Washington D.C.: Headquarters, Department of the Army, 2006); Bolger, *Savage Peace*, 278; Stewart, *The United States Army in Somalia*, 8.

[112]Bolger, *Savage Peace*, 277. According to Bolger, the Kenyans, were not shy in demanding reprisals in return for United States' acquisition of land in Kenya's Coast Province.

[113]Ibid.

[114]Ibid.

After becoming a lame duck on November 3, 1992, President Bush convened the

National Security Council's (NSC) Deputies Committee on November 20 to wrestle with options,

or series of actions, to deal with the now highly publicized humanitarian disaster in Somalia.[115]

The DoS "pressed for a larger U.S. role."[116] Secretary Albright said that the goal "was nothing

less than the restoration of an entire country as a proud, functioning and viable member of the

community of nations." [117] Providing the military's opposition, the Vice-Chairman of the Joint

Chiefs of Staff, Admiral David Jeremiah, "remained opposed to major intervention, as they had

been all along."[118] The military, led by General Collin Powell, felt there were too many questions

that no one asked: why was Somalia worthy of United States commitment? What national or vital

interests were at stake?[119] Many questions plagued the Bush Administration as described by

General Powell:

> What would constitute success; how could the United States avoid becoming caught in
> the tentacles of a confusing, several-sided civil war; would the American people support
> the effort? How many lives would it cost; how long would it last; how could the U.S.
> forces be extricated; and arguably the most important question, so what? Even if the
> United States-led a massive security and relief effort, what would prevent things in
> Somalia from sliding right back to business as usual within a few months after U.S.
> forces left?[120]

---

[115]Bolger, *Savage Peace*, 278-9. Described as a section tier of political, diplomatic, intelligence, and military leadership is the Deputies Committee.; George Herbert Walker Bush Presidential Library, "NSC/DC Meeting List, 1989-1993," The George Bush Presidential Library and Museum, http://bushlibrary.tamu.edu/research/pdfs/nsc_and_dc_meetings_1989-1992-declassified.pdf (accessed December 18, 2012). President Bush convened (at least) 23 White House-level meetings on Somalia between November 20, 1992 and January 12, 1993.

[116]Bolger, *Savage Peace*, 280.

[117]Meredith, *The Fate of Africa*, 478.

[118]Bolger, *Savage Peace*, 280.

[119]Ibid.

[120]This line of questioning supports what has become known as the "Powell Doctrine." This form of understanding required political leaders clearly defined the military end state prior to initiating military operations; General Powell himself was opposed to military interventions that

Although the aforementioned questions went unanswered by senior leaders in the U.S. Government, on November 25, 1992, President Bush approved the NSC's recommended course of action to deal with the Somalia problem. In a statement to the world, President Bush said, "our mission is humanitarian, but we will not tolerate armed gangs ripping off their own people, condemning them to death by starvation. [Our] troops have the authority to take whatever military action is necessary to safeguard the lives of our troops and [the Somalis]."[121] This speech informed the world of the U.S. Government's intentions for intervention in Somalia.

Interagency and Special Operations Forces Actions

Innately this problem was not solely a military or SOF issue, and the solution required multinational and interagency participation to be successful. The solution relied largely on the perception of the United States and the international community.[122] Presented with a series of options, the one President Bush chose was Operation Provide Hope. Within this operation, United States and UN efforts would focus on humanitarian assistance with limited military action.[123]

---

did not involve United States interests.; Bolger, *Savage Peace*, 280-1; The Observer, "Reluctant Warrior," The Guardian http://www.guardian.co.uk/world/2001/sep/30/usa.afghanistan (accessed January 5, 2013).

[121]George Bush, "Address to the Nation on the Situation in Somalia" (White House, Washington D.C., December 4, 1992), http://bushlibrary.tamu.edu/research/public_papers.php?id=5100&year=1992&month=12 (accessed January 31, 2013).

[122]"Perception often has a greater effect than reality in determining the success or failure of special operations. The forces must anticipate and counter hostile propaganda and disinformation while striving to enhance the perception of their mission by carefully integrating public affairs and PSYOP into their activities. There are problems with using PSYOP and public affairs to create perception; they attempt rather to correct misperceptions. Additionally, PSYOP and public affairs are separate by law. This may make coordination between the two difficult at best." Walter E. Kretchik, Robert F. Baumann, and John T. Fishel, *Invasion, Intervention, "Intervasion": A Concise History of the U.S. Army in Operation Uphold Democracy* (Fort Leavenworth, K.S.: U.S. Army Command and General Staff College Press, 1998), 116.

[123]Allard, *Somalia Operations* (Washington D.C.: National Defense University Press, 1995), 12. This course of action involved a 2-brigade plan (1-Army and 1-Marine).

In addition, on November 25, the acting U.S. Secretary of State, Lawrence Eagleburger delivered the U.S. Government's offer to the UN Secretary-General.[124] The offer advised the Secretary-General that the United States would be ready to take the lead in organizing and commanding multinational forces to establish conditions for successful humanitarian relief in Somalia.[125] After socializing the U.S. Government position with the security council, on December 3, 1992, UNSCR 794 was enacted, and gave contributing nations the go ahead to use "all means necessary" to establish a secure environment for humanitarian relief operations (under Chapter VII of the UN Charter).[126] On December 4, President Bush announced to the world that the United States-led UN intervention in Somalia "…would not be open-ended." By this, President Bush meant that U.S. military efforts would not last a day longer than necessary.[127] For military planners, very little discussed a military end state, or what factor(s) would constitute success for the U.S. President. The longer these questions remained unanswered, the longer they sat in a strategic vacuum. Although they were unable to clearly define the military conditions and establish assessment criteria for operations in Somalia, the DoS and the DoD advised President Bush that the conditions were ripe for intervention. The U.S. Government then proceeded to commit military forces in Somalia.

---

[124]United Nations, "Somalia - UNOSOM I: Background," United Nations, www.un.org/en/peacekeeping/missions/past/unosom1backgr2.html.

[125]Ibid.

[126]United Nations, "Somalia - UNOSOM II Mandate," United Nations http://www.un.org/en/peacekeeping/missions/past/unosom2mandate.html (accessed January 11, 2013); Department of Public Information, "United Nations Operation in Somalia II," United Nations (accessed January 5, 2013); Also referenced in Christopher L. Baggott, "A Leap Into The Dark: Crisis Action Planning For Operation Restore Hope" (MMAS Monograph, Command and General Staff College, 1996), 11.

[127]George Bush, "Address to the Nation on the Situation in Somalia" (White House, Washington D.C., December 4, 1992), http://bushlibrary.tamu.edu/research/public_papers.php?id=5100&year=1992&month=12 (accessed January 31, 2013).

Operation Restore Hope began December 8, 1992, under the direction of the Unified

Task Force (UNITAF).[128] Initially planned as an UN-led effort, the UNITAF was a multinational

force organized and led under a single United States military command.[129] The command

considered "all means necessary" to establish a secure environment for humanitarian relief

operations in Somalia.[130] Before SEALs were televised landing on the beaches in Mogadishu, the

military's interagency partners had already laid the diplomatic groundwork; engaging with the

Somali warlords in order to establish a ceasefire.[131] The overwhelming threat of defeat, coupled

with the progress made during negotiations between the two primary factions, resulted in a

reluctant peace among Somali warlords. This enabled the UNITAF to establish a brief respite

from hostilities within Somalia.[132] William R. Piekney, the Chief of the CIA's Africa Division,

alleged that the U.S. military deployed to Somalia without knowing much about the country,

stating, "We were their eyes and ears on the ground."[133] In an article published in *Parameters*,

---

[128]Allied forces included: some thirty-eight thousand soldiers from 23 different nations, for more information, see Montgomery, *US Forces in Somalia AAR* (Washington D.C.: Center of Military History, 2003); U.S. Department of the Army, *FM 3-06, Appendix C*, 2006 (Washington D.C.: Headquarters, Department of the Army, 2006).

[129]Montgomery, *US Forces in Somalia AAR* (Washington D.C.: Center of Military History, 2003); U.S. Department of the Army, *FM 3-06, Appendix C*, 2006 (Washington D.C.: Headquarters, Department of the Army, 2006).

[130]United Nations, "Somalia - UNOSOM II Mandate," United Nations http://www.un.org/en/peacekeeping/missions/past/unosom2mandate.html (accessed January 11, 2013).

[131]Stewart, *The United States Army in Somalia*, 9.; Montgomery, *US Forces in Somalia AAR* (Washington D.C.: Center of Military History, 2003), 6-7. Ambassador Oakley was given credit as the U.S. negotiator creating the ceasefire between the two factions (General Aidid and Ali Mahdi).

[132]Montgomery, *US Forces in Somalia AAR* (Washington D.C.: Center of Military History, 2003), 6-7.; Stewart, *The United States Army in Somalia*, 9.

[133]Vernon Loeb, "After-Action Report: Spying used to mean stealing another government's secrets, but what can spies achieve in a country with no government? In Somalia with the CIA, Garrett Jones and John Spinelli found out," *Washington Post*, February 27, 2000;

Garrett Jones illuminates that the working relationships between the military and the CIA was far from perfect, and that were several issues regarding chain of command and roles and authorities between the key players.[134] Despite having similar motivations for intervention, "little planning was done by the UN, and U.S. planning on behalf of the UN was not effectively integrated."[135] Amid this turmoil, SOF had the task of combining, sequencing, and proportionally implementing a variety of activities to accomplish the ever changing UN and US political objectives.[136]

Tactically, the Joint Special Operations Forces-Somalia was responsible for planning and conducting special operations in Somali to support all UNITAF humanitarian relief efforts.[137] However, with the lack of a clearly defined end state, the U.S. military forces concluded that progress towards security in Mogadishu required Aideed be neutralized.[138] Coalition military forces made difficult judgment calls when deciphering friendly from hostile forces in Somalia. Eventually, they developed a standard which became known as "the four No's": No technical, No visible weapons, No militia checkpoints (for tolls and other demands), and No bandits (warlord militia units)."[139] The deployed Soldiers had the authority to shoot first. Additionally, they were

---

This article is also available at: Special Operations, "The CIA in Somalia, 1993." SpecialOperations, http://www.specialoperations.com/Operations/Restore_Hope/CIA.htm (accessed December 15, 2012)..

[134]Garrett Jones, "Working with the CIA," *Parameters* XXXI, (Winter 2001-02): 28-39 http://www.carlisle.army.mil/usawc/Parameters/Articles/01winter/jones.htm.

[135]David Bentley and Robert Oakley, "Peace Operations: A Comparison of Somalia and Haiti," *Institute for National Strategic Studies*, no. 30 (1995); Special Operations, SpecialOperations, http://www.specialoperations.com/Operations/Restore_Hope/CIA.htm (accessed December 15, 2012).

[136]U.S. Department of the Army, *FM 3-06, Appendix C,* 2006 (Washington D.C.: Headquarters, Department of the Army, 2006).

[137]Stewart, *The United States Army in Somalia*, 7.

[138]Gray, *War, Peace and International Relations*, 225.

[139]Bolger, *Savage Peace*, 285-6

required to "read the moods of men whose language they did not speak."[140] It was not long after the initial arrival of military forces that "mission creep" settled in and began to permeate Operation Restore Hope.[141] The original intent of humanitarian assistance became a forgotten memory that became clouded by the dangerous realities of a volatile security environment. In peacekeeping operations, mission creep, where the objective of the operation changes as the operation develops, is a recipe for disaster.[142] The opposing view argues that Operation Restore Hope succeeded. The operation succeeded by bringing an end to mass starvation and the heavily armed UNITAF units quickly established security within their sectors.[143] As markets in populated areas reopened, travel throughout the country became more common, lending the security situation to some measure of normalcy; Operation Restore Hope was abandoned.

On March 26, 1993, UNOSOM II began with the enactment of UNSCR 814, four months after the United States-led multinational force (UNITAF) had begun, and less than six weeks before UNOSOM II was to take over.[144] The UNSCR 814 "considerably broadened" the United States and UN mission in Somalia.[145] As the Deputy of all UNISOM II forces in Somalia and commander of U.S. forces in Somalia, Major General Thomas M. Montgomery served under the United States Central Command Commander, General Joseph P. Hoar.[146] By October 1993,

---

[140]Gray, *War, Peace and International Relations*, 225.

[141]Stewart, *The United States Army in Somalia*, 9.

[142]Jan Angstrom and J.J. Widen, "Adopting a Recipe for Success: Modern Armed Forces and the Institutionalization of the Principles of War," *Comparative Politics* 31, no. 3 (July 16, 2012): 263-85.

[143]Stewart, *The United States Army in Somalia*, 9.

[144]Bentley and Oakley, "Peace Operations," 1.

[145]Stewart, *The United States Army in Somalia*, 9.

[146]Ibid.

UNISOM II consisted of sixteen thousand peacekeepers from twenty-one nations.[147] By mid-November, this number increased to 29,732 soldiers from twenty-nine nations; the arrival included an additional seventeen thousand U.S. personnel as a part of the U.S. Joint Task Force.[148] General Montgomery performed nation building as an addition to peacekeeping and to maintain a positive posture with the Somali people at large both within and outside of Mogadishu. Within Mogadishu, he saw that the Somali clans understood that the United States and coalition forces would continue to honor its commitment to protect the Somali people.[149]

Coalition forces identified Aideed's support system as the center of gravity for the hostile rebel faction. Composed of ground forces from the 75th Ranger Regiment, air assets from Task Force 160th, and members of the special forces Delta unit, U.S. Task Force (TF) Ranger, under the command of Major General Garrison, arrived in Mogadishu on August 26, 1993.[150] The mission of the TF included raids, cordon and searches, search and clears, aerial attacks, and reconnaissance operations.[151] Between August and September, TF Ranger conducted five successful surgical operations in Somalia; a sixth proved unsuccessful as the SOF element assaulted and restrained UN employees after receiving faulty intelligence.[152] Although very

---

[147]Montgomery, *US Forces in Somalia AAR* (Washington D.C.: Center of Military History, 2003), 9; Stewart, *The United States Army in Somalia*, 9.

[148]Ibid.

[149]Montgomery, *US Forces in Somalia AAR* (Washington D.C.: Center of Military History, 2003), 9; Stewart, *The United States Army in Somalia*, 9.

[150]Bolger, *Savage Peace*, 274.

[151]Center for Army Lessons Learned, "U.S. Army Operations in Support of UNOSOM II" (Fort Leavenworth, K.S.: U.S. Army Combined Arms Center, I-3-1.

[152]Art Pine and John M. Broder, "U.S. Faults Intelligence in Failed Somalia Raid," *Los Angeles Times*, August 31, 1993. http://articles.latimes.com/1993-08-31/news/mn-29737_1_clinton-administration (accessed February 1, 2013).

different from the humanitarian aims in the initial UN charter, these missions, now categorized by an increased use of firepower, resulted in higher civilian casualties.

Collaboration between the Interagency and Special Operations Forces

In Somalia, the United States needed a cohesive and effective body that could produce coordinated and continuous planning to drive timely actions. The dislocation of key U.S. Embassy personnel hamstrung interagency collaboration on United States efforts in Somalia. Forced to evacuate from the U.S. Embassy in Somalia on January 5, 1991, the U.S. Embassy in Mogadishu moved its operations to Nairobi, Kenya.[153] Madeleine Albright said in her memoirs that, "There was no U.S. Embassy staff in Mogadishu…lacking diplomatic front men, [military advisors] had to make [their] own arrangements."[154] Referring to the U.S. military forces, this problem did not go away.

From the beginning, there were two basic problems for United States and UN operational planners. The first problem was how to move enough essential supplies (food, water, medicine) into Somalia. The second problem was how to "provide security to protect the relief supplies from theft by bandits or confiscat[ed] by the clans and warring factions."[155] General Powell later stated that, "[the military] had a hard time getting clear guidance from the interagency process."[156] He said that while he received backchannel information, the military received

---

[153]During Operation Eastern Exit, 281 people (including eight Ambassadors, sixty-one Americans, and thirty-nine Soviets) were extracted from the U.S. Embassy in Mogadishu, for Ambassador Bishop's view of the situation, see U.S. Diplomacy, "Diplomats in Harms Way," http://www.usdiplomacy.org/history/service/jamesbishop.php (accessed February 1, 2013).

[154]Madeleine Albright and with Bill Woodward, *Madam Secretary* (New York, N.Y.: Miramax, 2003), 142; Bolger, *Savage Peace*, 274.

[155]Allard, *Somalia Operations*, 12.

[156]U.S. Congress. Senate, "Review of the Circumstances Surrounding the Ranger Raid on October 3-4, 1993 in Mogadishu," in *Committee on Armed Services* (Washington D.C.: United States Senate, 1995), 44.

"nothing from State."[157] Powell continued that, "[t]here were many meetings, but no results. It took too long to get a policy review accomplished."[158] The Congress found that diplomatic activity and military efforts were not well coordinated within the Clinton Administration or between the U.S. and UN.[159] In essence, the lapse in collaboration contributed to the dreadful disaster known by many as "Blackhawk Down" on October 3, 1993. The outcomes of the failed attempts to collaborate between the military and the interagency are too many to list in detail, but some key outcomes of the humanitarian crisis and U.S. military efforts provide useful considerations for future military and interagency operations in Somalia.

Outcomes

For the humanitarian crisis, the usual humanitarian relief organizations from CARE International, Save the Children, the United Nations Children's Fund, World Vision, and others operated in the country since the departure of the Somali dictator Siad Barre. Like the innocent victims of turmoil, however, these organizations could not function in the unstable and resource depleted environment. While it is difficult to say with certainty, "an estimated 25% of Somalia's six-million people died from starvation or disease."[160] Humanitarian operations require a significant level of planning at both the strategic and operational levels in order to be successful. The episode of Blackhawk Down provided useful lessons learned about the evolution of warfare and the necessity for integrated planning and collaboration.

---

[157]U.S. Congress. Senate, "Review of the Circumstances Surrounding the Ranger Raid on October 3-4, 1993 in Mogadishu,"44.

[158]Ibid.

[159]U.S. Congress. Senate, "Review of the Circumstances Surrounding the Ranger Raid on October 3-4, 1993 in Mogadishu," in *Committee on Armed Services* (Washington D.C.: United States Senate, 1995), 44.

[160]U.S. Department of the Army, *FM 3-06, Appendix C,* 2006 (Washington D.C.: Headquarters, Department of the Army, 2006).

At the strategic level, "what President Bush originally decided and what the Clinton Administration later did represents fundamental divergent approaches" in Somalia.[161] The United States and UN policies in Somalia were uncoordinated and unclear, and military operations were difficult to plan and conduct in combat.[162] The U.S. military "failed to assess and recognize critical [vulnerabilities] of their helicopters in an urban environment and the potential impact on their operations."[163] Furthermore, TF Ranger miscalculated the Somali's capacity to shoot down U.S. military helicopters, despite previous attempts by Somalis to use rocket-propelled grenades in earlier raids.[164]

Without clearly understanding or accepting what true success in Somalia required, the aftermath of Blackhawk Down forced the Clinton Administration on a U.S. Government exit strategy. The political objectives between the UN and United States did not match; the two were simply "coming to agreements." The UN was seeking a clear peacekeeping (noncombat military operations) mission, but instead, the United States established and handed over a peace enforcement (coercive use of military force) mission.[165] Peace operations, as opposed to more conventional military operations, frequently lack a traditional enemy. Additionally, they also tend to be highly ambiguous and are often subject to frequently changing political guidance.

As the policy objectives expanded the scope of United States involvement in Mogadishu, strategic and operational planners lost sight of the initial objectives. Without a clearly defined end state to conclude hostilities, missions in Somalia continued. What later became known as

---

[161]John R. Bolton, "Wrong Turn in Somalia," *Foreign Affairs* 73, no. i (1994): 56.

[162]Bolger, *Savage Peace*, 274.

[163]U.S. Department of the Army, *FM 3-06, Appendix C*, 2006 (Washington D.C.: Headquarters, Department of the Army, 2006).

[164]Ibid.

[165]Ibid.

"mission creep" entered into the planning and development of U.S. Government operations. In essence, assessments were not continuously informing military leaders on the progress of ongoing operations. To minimize the complexness of coordination, assessments would have taken into account any increases in organizations within the operating environment. It has been questioned whether the military or other interagency officials are responsible for conducting whole-of-government assessments. Regardless of the answer, few organizations within the United States have emerged to do so. While many organizations are uniquely capable of conducting such assessments, few understand what and how each other plan, and what assessment criteria went into planning.

Understanding the different cultures of organizational level planning, whether detailed or conceptual, can lead to a better fundamental understanding of the capabilities and capacities of each contributing organization. As many military officers have stressed to the DoS and the United States Agency for International Aid and Development do not conduct "detailed" planning. Inversely, their civilian counterparts would offer that diplomacy and development do not have "end states." Regardless of the type and level of planning, the coordination and collaboration among the organizations increases during the process of planning. In essence, this is the fundamental utility of integrating interagency and special operations forces. Without this level of planning, the government efforts become further hamstrung and broken.

Haiti (1994-1995)

Introduction to Haiti

This section introduces Haiti's geography, her and societal construct, as well as military and political issues leading to United States intervention in 1994. Before turning to an understanding of the operational environment, this section seeks to understand the divergent factors that contributed to understanding the operational environment. Located in the Caribbean Sea between Cuba and Puerto Rico, the island of Hispaniola is home to the small country of the

Dominican Republic and Haiti. Haiti occupies the western third of the island of Hispaniola and occupies 27,750 square kilometers of land, making it nearly the same size as Maryland.[166] Haiti borders the Atlantic Ocean to the north, the Caribbean Sea to the west and south, and shares 360 kilometers of land with the Dominican Republic to the east. In the early 1990s, minor skirmishes over border disputes between Haiti and the Dominican Republic were problematic, but since the 2010 earthquake, these issues have diminished.[167] Haiti also neighbors a vital sea route northeast of the Panama Canal, which is of strategic importance economically to many nations transiting this route daily. Figure 2 provides a basic map of the region.

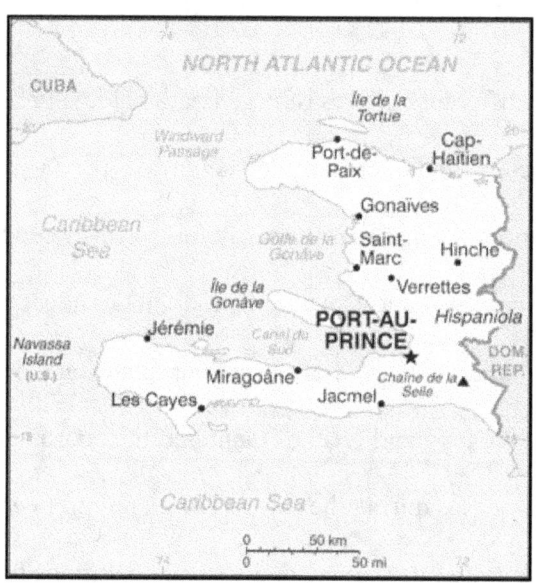

Figure 2: Haiti.

Source: Central Intelligence Agency, "Central America And Caribbean: Haiti https://www.cia.gov/library/publications/the-world-factbook/maps/maptemplate_ha.html (accessed February 7, 2013).

---

[166]Helen Chapin Metz, *Dominican Republic and Haiti: Country Studies* (Washington, D.C.: Library of Congress, 2001), 8; U.S. Central Intelligence Agency, "The World Factbook," Central Intelligence Agency http://nodedge.com/ciawfb/ (accessed Feburary 7, 2013).

[167]Metz, *Dominican Republic and Haiti* (Washington, D.C.: Library of Congress, 2001), 8.

Haitians have a common language and one of the richest cultural heritages in the world.[168] For many Haitians, life is characterized by poverty, hard work, simplicity, community, and whenever possible, celebration.[169] Suffering and hardship, and with issues such as poor healthcare, malnutrition, and a lack of education also characterize life for many Haitians. "Decades of poverty, environmental degradation, violence, instability, and dictatorship," have left Haiti as the poorest nation in the Americas.[170] Additionally, Haitians have a profound attachment to Voodoo and Catholicism. A Haitian folk expression states that, "Haiti is 90 percent Catholic and 100 percent voodoo."[171] As the national religion, Voodoo is a blend of different beliefs that Haitians celebrate through song, dance, and prayer.[172]

Historically, Haiti has been a strategic interest to the United States. The opening of the Panama Canal in 1914 elevated Haiti's strategic importance to the U.S. Government as American officials sought to counter Germany's perceived attempts to expand its influence into the Caribbean.[173] In July 1915, political instability in Haiti prompted the U.S. Government to send the U.S. Marine Corps to Haiti to ensure the safety and security of the Haitian people. According to one widely read study, a Marine Corps veteran assessed that United States efforts were

---

[168]Roseline Ng Cheong-Lum and Leslie Jermyn, *Cultures of the World: Haiti* (Tarrytown, NY: Marshall Cavendish Benchmark, 2005), 63.

[169]Ibid.

[170]British Broadcasting Corporation, "Haiti Country Profile," British Broadcasting Corporation http://news.bbc.co.uk/2/hi/americas/country_profiles/1202772.stm (accessed February 7, 2013).

[171]Cheong-Lum and Jermyn, *Cultures of the World: Haiti*, 78.

[172]Ibid.

[173]Kretchik, Baumann, and Fishel, *Invasion, Intervention, "Intervasion": A Concise History*, 7.

constrained by an appreciation for Haitian culture before the 1915 intervention.[174] As a show of the lack in understanding, several U.S. Marine Corps trainees graduated from boot camp and learned about the Haitian culture on the job, while in Haiti.[175] In fact, "[t]he Marines insisted on establishing the Jim Crow standards of the American South as soon as they settled in."[176] The effects of not understanding Haitian culture, however, led to the U.S. military aggravating underlying racial tensions between two social classes identified as the large and impoverished dark-skinned class and the small wealthy, and predominantly lighter-skinned social and economic Haitian elites.[177] A paper published at Concordia University suggested that the apparent benefits derived from United States intervention in 1915 also contributed to the existing problems in Haiti today.[178]

In March 1987, the Haitians adopted a constitution that called for presidential and legislative elections. However, military factions looking to maintain power in Haiti conducted terrorist attacks at polling sites in November subsequently postponing the scheduled elections. Unable to stall the democratic movement, however, voters elected a parliament and a president in

---

[174]Kretchik, Baumann, and Fishel, *Invasion, Intervention, "Intervasion": A Concise History*, 7.

[175]Hans Schmidt, *The U.S. Occupation of Haiti* (New Brunswick, N.J.: Rutgers University Press, 1971), 136; As found in: Kretchik, Baumann, and Fishel, *Invasion, Intervention, "Intervasion": A Concise History*, 8.

[176]*Jim Crow* refers to the Jim Crow laws between 1876 and 1965, which mandated separation in public facilities between *whites* and *blacks* in the United States. Examples of segregation included (but not limited to) education, restaurants, drinking fountains, etc.; Schmidt, *The U.S. Occupation of Haiti*, 136; as found in: Kretchik, Baumann, and Fishel, *Invasion, Intervention, "Intervasion": A Concise History*, 8.

[177]In 1993, the white and mulatto elite comprised only 4.5% of the total population, but they controlled nearly 95% of the country's economy and all of the political power, for an understanding of Haitian society, see Cheong-Lum and Jermyn, *Cultures of the World: Haiti*.

[178]David Campbell, "The Social and Cultural Impacts of the United States Occupation of the People of Haiti (1915-1934)," (Concordia University, 2007), 2.

January 1988. The rivaling military factions would not cede power so easily and in June, and again in September, military coups overthrew the seated president and established military control. The back and forth struggle ended in March 1990, as protestors ousted the military regime. In December, the Haitians elected Jean-Bertrand Aristide, who became the first democratically elected president of Haiti, ending years of military rule. Haiti joined the global trend toward democratic governance, but this episode would only be a brief moment of calm for the nascent democracy.[179]

Understanding the Operational Environment

The operational environment describes the circumstances affecting the situation, as depicted in Haiti, beginning in 1991. During this time, political instability reigned and the refugee problem was getting worse. The mass migration and catastrophic malnutrition of the Haitian people led to internal U.S. Government discourse on how to deal with the socially and politically unstable Haiti. In February 1991, President Aristide took office after winning two-thirds of the Haitian vote in an internationally monitored election, and made Lieutenant General Raoul Cedras Commander-in-Chief of the Haitian armed forces.[180] With his presidency came reforms that created opposition from the political and military elite.[181] President Aristide's term did not last the five continuous years as the constitution specified. On September 29, 1991, an armed rebellion, led by Lieutenant General Cedras, successfully overthrew President Aristide. Aristide,

---

[179] "Haiti," *Worldmark Encyclopedia of Nations*, Encyclopedia.com. http://www.encyclopedia.com/doc/1G2-2586700161.html (accessed on March 14, 2013).

[180] Adam B. Siegel, *The Intervasion of Haiti* (Alexandria, VA: Center for Naval Analysis, 1996), 4; James Dobbins, John G. McGinn, Keith Crane, Seth G. Jones, Rollie Lai, Andrew Rathmell, Rachel Swanger, and Anga Timilsina, *America's Role in Nation-Building: From Germany to Iraq* (Santa Monica, CA: RAND, 2003), 71.

[181] President Aristide attempted to institute retirements for senior military officers, civilian control of the military and police, corruption reduction, and punishments for political and military leaders who were previously involved in human rights abuses.

subsequently departed the island of Hispaniola in search of international assistance in Washington D.C., not far from the White House.[182] Between his departure and his reemergence in October 1994, thousands of Haitians were killed.

During President Bush's Administration, it was understood that whole-of-government approaches to complex problems were essential for national security. However, the use of U.S. military force to restore democracy in Haiti was considered the last resort on the range of United States policy options.[183] Dick Cheney, then Secretary of Defense, asked General Colin Powell, then Chairman of the Joint Chiefs of Staff, what he thought about using military force in Haiti, General Powell replied, "We can take the country over in an afternoon with a company or two of Marines."[184] Getting out of Haiti would be the problem. Powell did not intend to support an invasion just to restore a questionable democracy devoid of democratic institutions or conventions.[185] While the NSC favored the use of military force, DoD remained against it.[186] Publically, U.S. Government policy was to use diplomatic means to return President Aristide to

---

[182]Warren Christopher, *In the Stream of History: Shaping Foreign Policy for a New Era* (Stanford, CA: Stanford University Press, 1998), 174.

[183]Warren Christopher, *In the Stream of History*, 178.

[184]Dale R. Herspring, *The Pentagon and the Presidency: Civil-Military Relations from FDR to George W. Bush* (Lawrence, KS: University Press of Kansas, 2005), 351.

[185]Ibid.

[186]Margaret Daly Hayes and Gary F. Weatley, *Interagency and Political-Military Dimensions of Peace Operations: Haiti - A Case Study* (Washington D.C.: National Defense University Press, 1996), 14-15.

power.[187] Interagency planning was further complicated when President Clinton stated that the Administration would consider the use of force in Haiti.[188]

Between 1991 and 1994, social and political instability reigned in Haiti for a population of nearly seven million, eleven percent of Haitian children were malnourished and dying. Nearly nine percent of the Haiti's population was HIV positive. To support this social dilemma, Haiti employed only 810 doctors (nearly 8,540 patients per physician).[189] By comparison, in 1990, the United States had 615,400 licensed physicians for a population of 248.71M (nearly 385 patients per physician).[190] The Haitians were in need of serious humanitarian assistance.[191] Also during this period, thirty thousand Haitians found refuge in the Dominican Republic, an upwards of three hundred thousand were displaced within Haiti, and some 68,500 Haitians were assessed to have fled Haiti in small boats.[192] Many surfaced on Florida beaches, while many others were not as fortunate. The "boat people," or the refugees, were apparently the problem for the United States.[193]

---

[187]M argaret Daly Hayes and Gary F. Weatley, *Interagency and Political-Military Dimensions of Peace Operations: Haiti - A Case Study* (Washington D.C.: National Defense University Press, 1996), 14-15.

[188]Ibid.

[189]For additional statistics, see Schulz and Marcella. Donald E. Schulz and Gabriel Marcella, "Reconciling the Irreconcilable: The troubled outlook for U.S. policy toward Haiti" (Carlisle Barracks, PA: Strategic Studies Institute, U.S. Army War College, 1994), 3-5.

[190]U.S. Census Bureau, "Table 165-6. Physicians by Sex and Specialty: 1980-1992," http://www.census.gov/compendia/statab/2012/tables/12s0165.pdf (accessed February 16, 2013).

[191]Donald E. Schulz and Gabriel Marcella *Reconciling the Irreconcilable: The troubled outlook for U.S. policy toward Haiti* (Carlisle Barracks, PA: Strategic Studies Institute, U.S. Army War College, 1994), 3-5.

[192]Dobbins, McGinn, Crane, Jones, Lai, Rathmell, Swanger, and Timilsina, *America's Role in Nation-Building*, 72.

[193]William J. Clinton, "The President's Radio Address," The American Presidency Project, http://www.clintonlibrary.gov/assets/storage/Research-

American Pulitzer Prize-winning journalist, author, and historian, David Halberstam viewed Haiti as an "open sore, a nation that produced a constant flood of refugees who sailed to the United States in a sad little armada of homemade boats under the most desperate circumstances."[194] Under the Bush Administration, the U.S. Coast Guard interdicted the fleeing Haitians and sent them back to Haiti. However, before the Clinton Administration even took office, they saw this as criminal and inhumane and spoke out publically about his opposition to President Bush's interdictions. As Halberstam points out, Clinton quickly changed his rhetoric after receiving intelligence reports and pictures from the CIA that showed thousands of Haitians tearing off the roofs to their houses and turning them into boats to sail to America.[195] The CIA assessed that, "The United States could expect as many as two hundred thousand refugees."[196] While there was no significant national security threat that necessitated U.S. military force, the humanitarian situation and looming immigration crisis was enough to cause President Clinton to react, but not before four Haitian corpses, including two children, were found on two South Florida beaches.[197]

Less than one month after General Cedras had taken power, the UN called for the suspension of international aid to Haiti and to freeze Haitian Government assets internationally.[198] United States citizens and business firms were prohibited from sending

---

AV/audio/1994/DEC/PP_ROTP_RadioAddress_17Dec1994.mp3 (accessed February 5, 2013).

[194]David Halberstam, *War in a Time of Peace: Bush, Clinton, and the Generals* (New York, NY: Simon and Schuster, 2001), 195.

[195]Ibid.

[196]Halberstam, *War in a Time of Peace*, 269.

[197]Christopher, *In the Stream of History*, 175; Mike Clary, "Bodies of Four Hatians Wash Ashore in Florida," *Los Angeles Times*, February 9, 1994, http://articles.latimes.com/1994-02-09/news/mn-20900_1_haitian-migrants (accessed February 12, 2013).

[198]Sarah Bermeo, "Clinton and Coercive Diplomacy: A Study of Haiti," Woodrow

financial transactions to Haiti in support of the ongoing turmoil. Politically, the international community employed economic sanctions against the Haitian Government and threatened the use of military force to remove General Cedras from power.[199] From the United States perspective, the period between October 1991 and September 1994 was a period of peacemaking, that is to say a period of mediation and negotiation designed to bring hostile parties to negotiation.[200] Indeed, diplomatic efforts were underway despite the deployments of military forces and the conduct of maritime interception operations, sanction enforcement, refugee recovery, and other various types of displays of force.[201]

By the summer of 1994, the refugee problem was getting worse. Between July 3 and 4, the U.S. Coast Guard intercepted over six thousand refugees attempting to flee Haiti for what might have been a better life in the United States.[202] Additionally, on July 31, UNSCR 940 authorized six thousand military personnel to use "all necessary means" to facilitate the departure of General Cedras' military regime and restore the democratically elected, President Aristide.[203]

Wilson School of Public and International Affairs (Princeton, NJ: Princeton University, 2001), 5.

[199]Dobbins, McGinn, Crane, Jones, Lai, Rathmell, Swanger, and Timilsina, *America's Role in Nation-Building*, 71.

[200]Siegel, *The Intervasion of Haiti*, 8; Olara A. Otunnu and Michael W. Doyle, *Peacemaking and Peacekeeping for the New Century* (Lanham: Rowman & Littlefield Publishers, 1998), 2.

[201]Siegel, *The Intervasion of Haiti*, 8.

[202]Christopher, *In the Stream of History*, 177.

[203]U.S. Department of State Dispatch, "Background Notes: Haiti," Bureau of Public Affairs http://dosfan.lib.uic.edu/ERC/briefing/dispatch/1995/html/Dispatchv6no24.html (accessed February 4, 2013); Embassy of Haiti in Washington D.C., "Key Dates in Haiti's History," Embassy of Haiti www.haiti.org/images/stories/pdf/key_dates.pdf (accessed February 4, 2013); Dobbins, McGinn, Crane, Jones, Lai, Rathmell, Swanger, and Timilsina, *America's Role in Nation-Building*, 74.

This resolution was the authority that the U.S. Government needed to nest the international community in support of a United States intervention in Haiti.[204]

Key Players

At the strategic level, key players leading up to United States intervention included the international television networks, the "Boat People," and the U.S. President. International television networks were quick to respond to the Haitian crises as "the CNN effect" heightened global perception on the security and humanitarian issues. Given a presidential campaign pledge from then-Governor Bill Clinton, the security threat posed to the United States worsened as the victims of turmoil in Haiti sought refuge and humanitarian relief within the United States. Still under pressure from the Blackhawk Down debacle in Somalia, President Clinton hoped for an easy way to fix the international community's perception that the United States could be defeated through asymmetrical means. In essence, the United States ability to understand the capabilities of key international and intergovernmental players effectively integrated planning efforts.[205]

The United States became more interested in the situation in Haiti after the media exposed the atrocities taking place in Haiti to the American public. According to an article published by Margaret Belknap in *Parameters*, the United States military initially planned to incorporate the media into its operations. "Reporters were given access to top-secret plans and information for the operation prior to the planned invasion. David Wood, a seasoned national security correspondent for *Newhouse News*, was assigned a seat on the command and control

---

[204]Christopher, *In the Stream of History*, 179. Then-UN Ambassador Madeleine Albright was the forerunner for the U.S. Government in advocating UN intervention in Haiti.

[205]James F. Dobbins, "Haiti: A Case Study in Post Cold-War Peacekeeping," *Institute for the Study of Diplomacy* II, no. I (October 1995): 5. Ambassador Dobbins believed that there needs to be a close integration of diplomatic, military, humanitarian, and economic instruments of power.

aircraft that would oversee the operation."[206] While many of Wood's peers were inadequately

attired for an invasion, some wearing shorts and sneakers, Wood wore his fatigues and flack

jacket ready to run into Haiti with the first wave of U.S. troops. An American Broadcasting

Company news cameraman agreed that some correspondents were not prepared for a combat

situation as they showed up with suitcases.[207] Regardless of their attire, "the news media's

pervasive presence in Haiti pressured the Clinton Administration to expand, at least slightly, the

parameters of the operation and become more involved than it had planned in protecting Haitians

from violence by other Haitians."[208]

The American people became more interested in Haiti given the country's geographic

proximity to the United States. This proximity influenced the reality of the situation beyond the

borders on the Island of Hispaniola. Daily non-stop flights from Port-au-Prince and New York

and Miami coupled with the ability to travel by small boats to the United States largely influenced

this reality. The Center for Strategic and International Studies reported that this interaction

between the two countries linked the United States and Haitian interests.[209] The massive

migration of Haitians eventually forced the U.S. Government to make a decision about the fleeing

Haitians. "The media focused its narrative on the fact that a military dictator controlled Haiti

while the country was falling deeper and deeper into economic ruin enabling, and the Haitian

---

[206]Margaret H. Belknap, "The CNN Effect: Strategic Enabler or Operational Risk?," *Parameters* XXXII (Autumn 2002): 106.

[207]Jacqueline E. Sharkey, "The Shallow End of the Pool?," *American Journalism Review*, (1994) www.ajr.org/article.asp?id=1580 (accessed February 18, 2013).

[208]Warren P. Strobel, *Late-Breaking Foreign Policy: The News Media's Influence on Peace Operations* (Washington D.C.: United States Institute of Peace, 1997), 109.

[209]Ernest H. Preeg, *The Haitian Dilemma: A Case Study in Demographics, Development, and U.S. Foreign Policy* (Washington, D.C.: Center for Strategic and International Studies, 1996), 10-11.

military to forcefully takeover the legitimate government of Haiti."[210] The U.S. Army Command and General Staff College authored a historical analysis of Operation Uphold Democracy, which assessed that the United States intercepted nearly twenty thousand Haitian refugees at sea from mid-June to early-July in 1994.[211] Additionally, the U.S. Coast Guard was returning refugees to Haiti at a rate of over six hundred people per day.[212] With respect to national interests, the geographical proximity between the United States and Haiti blurred the national boundaries; what was necessary in Haiti was also necessary to the American people. Coupled with an election year, the humanitarian situation in Haiti was a topic for not only the American people, but also the U.S. Presidential election.[213]

At the operational level, the key players were identified once the United States committed to military action. According to George Stephanopoulos, the NSC met on September 7, 1994, to discuss the invasion plan.[214] During this meeting, President Clinton's Chairman of the Joint Chiefs of Staff, General Shalikashvili, briefed the NSC and the President who served in a rare appearance as the principal in the meeting. At the end of the briefing the President said, without hedging or hesitation, "It's a good plan; let's go."[215] On September 15, President Clinton declared

---

[210]Brent P. Goddard, "Military Peacekeeping Operations in Haiti" (Marine Corps University Command and Staff College, 1997).

[211]Kretchik, Baumann, and Fishel, *Invasion, Intervention, "Intervasion": A Concise History*, 57.

[212]Ibid.

[213]Preeg, *The Haitian Dilemma, 58.*

[214]George Stephanopoulos, *All Too Human: A Political Education* (Boston, MA: Little, Brown, 1999), 306. Stephanopoulos served as President Clinton's Senior Advisor on Policy and Strategy and de facto Press Secretary.

[215]Ibid. Stephanopoulos states in his book that much of the discussion in the NSC meeting centered on how to present the plan to Congress, and whether or not to present the plan to them prior to committing U.S. military forces.

"all diplomatic initiatives were exhausted and that the United States with twenty other countries would form a multinational force." [216] As U.S. military forces were withdrawing from Somalia, some of the same military planners were planning for two options to resolve the vexing problem in Haiti. These two options included either a peaceful military intervention, or a quick and decisive military invasion. Of the two options, President Clinton initially selected a modified hybrid of the two plans.

On September 15, 1994, President Clinton made the case for intervention in an address directed at the existing Haitian military regime. In his address, President Clinton said, "The message of the United States to the Haitian dictators is clear. Your time is up. Leave now or we will force you from power."[217] Two days later President Clinton explained the strategic reasoning for intervention in a radio address to the world.[218] He said that the United States goals in Haiti would be limited to, "stopping the horrible atrocities, affirming that the United States keeps its commitments, securing the United States borders by averting the flow of thousands of refugees away from the United States, and preserving the stability of democracy in the western hemisphere."[219]

With the invasion scheduled for September 19, the United States had time for a single, last chance effort to resolve the situation peacefully. On behalf of President Clinton, former-President Jimmy Carter, Senator Sam Nunn, and then former-Chairman of the Joint Chiefs of Staff, Colin Powell, arrived in Haiti near-midday in an attempt to negotiate a peaceful transition

---

[216]Embassy of Haiti in Washington D.C., Embassy of Haiti, www.haiti.org/images/stories/pdf/key_dates.pdf (accessed February 4, 2013).

[217]Christopher, *In the Stream of History*, 180.

[218]Clinton, 1994. The American Presidency Project, http://www.clintonlibrary.gov/assets/storage/Research-AV/audio/1994/DEC/PP_ROTP_RadioAddress_17Dec1994.mp3 (accessed February 5, 2013).

[219]Ibid.

of power with General Cedras.[220] This powerful delegation had thirty-six hours to convince

General Cedras to resign peacefully, before United States forces commenced the invasion.

President Clinton hoped that the trio could convince the Haitian regime to peacefully step down

before United States occupation.[221] The window for diplomacy was closing rapidly on the U.S.

Government delegation, as airborne units had departed Fort Bragg in North Carolina in route to

overthrow the Haitian regime. At the last possible moment, President Clinton received a call from

former-President Carter telling him to call off the invasion; General Cedras would go peacefully.

Interagency and Special Operations Forces Actions

The President of the United States wanted the restoruction of the politically elected

government and stability from the humanitarian situation in Haiti. At the operational level, the

focus became to enable a safe and stable environment to facilitate the return of the democratically

elected government.[222] Conventional units and SOF were given the green light to conduct peace

operations in Haiti following former-President Carter's success in convincing General Cedras to

leave peacefully. Major ground forces involved in the operation consisted of the 82nd Airborne

Division and a Joint Special Operations Task Force (JSOTF). The JSOTF was composed of Army

Rangers, Army Special Forces, Navy SEALs, and helicopter support from the 160th SOAR.[223]

SOF operations in Haiti were used to achieve the president's strategic goals. This section will

focus on the actions of the U.S. Army Special Forces, CA, and the PSYOP units to remove the

---

[220]The U.S. deligation was initially requested by former-President Carter.

[221]Halberstam, *War in a Time of Peace*, 281.

[222]Siegel, *The Intervasion of Haiti*, 2.

[223]Christopher, *In the Stream of History*, 178.

impediment of enabling a stable environment in order to facilitate the return of the democratically elected government.[224]

On September 20, the United States began to deploy U.S. Army Special Forces teams throughout the countryside. Supported by CA support teams, Special Forces controlled the countryside to win the hearts and minds of the Haitian populations; many of which were not aware that the United States was present in Haiti.[225] Unlike their Special Forces counterparts, at the time, conventional military forces did not have the capability to operate in the countryside. Special Forces teams had long-range communications capability, specialized weapons, and specialized medical capability to enable their capabilities to perform in the rural areas of Haiti.[226] Despite U.S. military presence in most areas of Haiti, Haitian soldiers continued to beat demonstrators in an effort to maintain control over the population. Special Forces were successful in adapting to the local customs, traditions, and conditions and looked to build and leverage the relationships with local leaders in Haiti. These units began establishing contacts with local leaders as they explained the nature of the United States mission and simultaneously enlisting the local leaderships cooperation and support for the UN mission.[227] Generally, Special Forces provided order in the interior of Haiti, but there were instances where they directly assisted local authorities.[228]

---

[224]Kretchik, Baumann, and Fishel, *Invasion, Intervention, "Intervasion": A Concise History*, 143.

[225]Ibid., 143-144.

[226]Kenneth E. Tovo, "Special Forces' Missions Focus For The Future" (Monograph, U.S. Army Command and General Staff College, 1995), 30-36.

[227]U.S. Department of Defense, Joint Publication 3-08*: Interagency Coordination During Joint Operations,* 1996 (Washington D.C.: Headquarters, The Joint Chiefs of Staff 1996), I-3.

[228]Tucker and Lamb, *United States Special Operations Forces*, 99. One such instance saw the delivery of a Haitian child by U.S. Special Forces Solders.

In the wake of successful diplomatic negotiations between the United States and Haiti, both conventional and SOF forces understood that strategic U.S. Government leaders would require the military to contribute to building a stable environment as a means to facilitate the transfer of political power back to Haiti's democratically elected president. Additionally, given Haitian perceptions of the role of United States and multinational forces in Haiti, the information campaign would be essential to set the conditions to enable military missions.[229] U.S. military CA teams conducted assessments early in the operation to develop a plan for military assistance to nation building. These assessments defined the military projects in support of the political objectives.[230] When funding for CA projects ran out, the military quickly assessed that the reconstruction plan was beyond what was financially sustainable. Since long-term stability is enhanced by CA projects, it would appear that the long-term stability missions suffered from short-term tactical success. Since most of the CA projects were generally beyond the capabilities of organic military units, officers frequently requested CA assistance through the interagency processes.[231] One U.S. military officer surmised that for each organization operating in Haiti, there was an accompanying "synchronization matrix, a decision matrix, for bringing in the political plans, for bringing in the economic plans, for bringing in the interagency requirements."[232]

---

[229]Kretchik, Baumann, and Fishel, *Invasion, Intervention, "Intervasion": A Concise History*, 125.

[230]U.S. Department of State, "U.S. Relations with Haiti," Bureau of Western Hemisphere Affairs, http://www.state.gov/r/pa/ei/bgn/1982.htm (accessed February 4, 2012, 2012).

[231]Kretchik, Baumann, and Fishel, *Invasion, Intervention, "Intervasion": A Concise History*, 112-115.

[232]Phillip G. Pattee, "Special Operations Forces and Nonstate Actors in Operation Uphold Democracy: A Case Study" (U.S. Army Command and General Staff College, 1996), 100.

A key enabler that was synchronized across numerous units' areas during the United States intervention in Haiti were U.S. Army PSYOP teams. The execution of the PSYOP campaign commenced in advance of ground operations. In late August, the U.S. Air Force conducted a leaflet drop in the vicinity of St. More, Haiti. A typical leaflet theme displayed the words "democracy," "prosperity," "opportunity," "education," and "law," overlying a drawing of three persons moving into the sunlight."[233] Additional PSYOP techniques and tools for disseminating these themes included traditional methods such as, radios, television, handbills, loudspeakers, and leaflets, but also innovative promotion such as, t-shirts, billboards, and buttons.[234] This form of tactical PSYOP generally consisted of two-to-four person teams carrying loudspeakers with taped messages. Spoken in Creole, these messages served to prevent further violence by demanding the immediate surrender of hostile forces.[235]

Collaboration between the Interagency and Special Operations Forces

Two issues presented problems for U.S. Government operations in Haiti, and both had to do with organizational understanding. The first problem was due to a lapse in close interagency cooperation, or even accepted channels for coordination – this often left military planners working in a vacuum. Interagency collaboration for the United States efforts in Haiti was not hamstrung on a grand scale. However, at the operational level planners and leaders lacked an understanding of the divergent organizational cultures and organizations located in Haiti. Every United States organization involved in Haiti "were all planning their own participation in the

---

[233]Kretchik, Baumann, and Fishel, *Invasion, Intervention, "Intervasion": A Concise History*, 125.

[234]James C. Boisselle, "Communicating the Vision: Psychological Operations in Operation Uphold Democracy" (Research paper, U.S. Army Command and General Staff College, March 3, 1996).

[235]Kretchik, Baumann, and Fishel, *Invasion, Intervention, "Intervasion": A Concise History*, 126.

Haiti operation, there was little operational level coordination between agencies."[236] Given the fact that there was "little interaction between Washington-based agencies and ongoing planning by the military outside Washington…interagency coordination at the tactical level did not take place until troops were on the ground in Haiti."[237]

According to doctrine in 1993, the goal of interagency coordination was to develop and promote the unity-of-effort needed to accomplish specific missions.[238] These missions commanded coordination and integration from intra-government organizations whose goals, policies, procedures, and decision-making processes differed. This difference led to disjointed planning and could not achieve the synchronized approach desired of operational planning.[239] Many planners did not receive training or education on the roles and responsibilities of contributing joint, interagency, and multinational organizations.[240] In an interview, a U.S. Army officer reflected on the idea that, "Each organization has core values that they will not

---

[236]Hayes and Weatley, *Interagency and Political-Military Dimensions of Peace Operations: Haiti - A Case Study*, 16.

[237]Ibid, 14-15.

[238]Michael L. Sullivan, Commander, 16th MP Brigade interview with LTC Charles Cureton, November 8, 1994, ed., Cynthia L. Hayden, *Oral History Interviews: Operation Uphold Democracy*, (*Port-au-Prince, Haiti: XVIII Airborne Corps*).

[239]Edward C. Short, Special Operations Forces LNO to JTF 190 interview with CPT Thomas G. Ziek, October 6, 1994, ed., Cynthia L. Hayden, *Oral History Interviews: Operation Uphold Democracy*, (*Port-au-Prince, Haiti*), 415.

[240]Hayes and Weatley, *Interagency and Political-Military Dimensions of Peace Operations: Haiti - A Case Study*, 14-15.

compromise."[241] With this lack in understanding, workable compromises were necessary to integrate all of the elements of power.[242]

The second problem was uniquely internal to the DoD given that, "the working relationship between [Special Operations Forces] and conventional forces operating in Port-au-Prince was not always smooth."[243] Differences in training and culture divided the two from achieving a common perspective on the issues in Haiti.[244] At times, conventional units were unaware of what was happening in the countryside where SOF units were operating. Occasionally conventional units were surprised to encounter SOF units in the rural areas of Haiti. "Soldiers who have operated in both conventional and SOF domains attributed the intra-organizational differences in military cultures and the misperceptions between the two, as to the reasons for the divide.[245] In one instance, U.S. Army Special Forces Soldiers taught Haitian soldiers to "do the wave."[246] Conventional forces perceived this gesture as an act of disrespect. An officer from the conventional unit would later file charges against Soldiers from the U.S. Special Forces unit.[247]

As with most operations, maintaining operations security was critically significant. There were information silos among the various headquarters that controlled military activity

---

[241]Eric I. Mitchell, Civil Affairs Public Health Officer JTF 190, interview with MAJ Christopher Clark, October 10, 1994, ed., Cynthia L. Hayden, *Oral History Interviews: Operation Uphold Democracy*, (*Port-au-Prince, Haiti: XVIII Airborne Corps*), 134.

[242]John P. Lewis, U.S. Army Infantry, J-5 JTF 190, interview with MAJ Christopher Clark, October 18, 1994, ed., Cynthia L. Hayden, *Oral History Interviews: Operation Uphold Democracy*, (*Port-au-Prince, Haiti: XVIII Airborne Corps*), 222.

[243]Kretchik, Baumann, and Fishel, *Invasion, Intervention, "Intervasion": A Concise History*, 120.

[244]Ibid.

[245]Ibid.

[246]Ibid., 121.

[247]Ibid.

throughout the country, and at times, this compartmentalization was occurring within the same headquarters as well. Planners within one cell did not share information with anyone outside their own compartment. Thus, as Haiti would have it, "compartmentalized planning frustrated many planners who needed information to de-conflict problems and work through the complexities of the operation."[248] In the initial planning phases, a lack of information flow led to coordination and collaboration problems, although reporters were able to obtain top-secret information without much difficulty.[249] Ironically, for many military planners, it would take up to six months to obtain approval for a top-secret clearance, which prohibited planners with the necessary skillsets from participating in the initial planning for Haiti.[250]

Outcomes

Haiti, as an economically strategic location, became an agenda item for senior leadership with the potential rise of a political faction that may not have been friendly to United States interests in the region. Compounded with the media coverage of the refugees landing on the South Florida beaches, this issue resonated within the communities of many Americans who began to voice concern over the President's foreign policy and had severe domestic implications. Backed by strong domestic support, President Clinton was able to garner international support in the form of a military coalition and economic sanctions to remove General Cedras from power. President Clinton was quite effective at using diplomacy and the threat of war to his advantage to achieve his initial political objective, reinstating the democratically elected President in Haiti.

<hr>

[248]U.S. Department of Defense, Joint Publication 3-08: *Interagency Coordination During Joint Operations,* 1996 (Washington D.C.: Headquarters, The Joint Chiefs of Staff, 1996).

[249]Kretchik, Baumann, and Fishel, *Invasion, Intervention, "Intervasion": A Concise History,* 46-47.

[250]Ibid., 47.

CASE STUDY SYNTHESIS

The purpose of this section is to conduct a cross analysis, or synthesis of the two case studies previously examined. This section is comprised of three primary subsections, a review of the findings from each case study, and a synthesis highlighting the validity of the monograph's hypothesis. This hypothesis believes that collaborative approaches will be necessary for the future, and because of this, interagency and SOF communities require an evolution in interagency collaboration. Following this section, the monograph will conclude with observations and recommendations for senior leaders.

Somalia

A review of Somalia illustrates that whole-of-government approaches to complex problems are essential for United States national security. Since 1991, violence and corruption, coupled with drought and famine, led to a U.S. Government decision to provide security and humanitarian assistance in Somalia. The key players leading up to United States intervention in Somalia included international television networks, the U.S. President, DoS diplomats, and senior military decision-makers at the Pentagon. Interagency collaboration in Somalia was restrained by the dislocation of key U.S. Embassy personnel. Lacking in country diplomats, the interagency process, according to General Powell, produced no results. Coordination and collaboration among the interagency and SOF would have increased the effectiveness of planning. Additionally, U.S. strategic leaders did not define planning assessment criteria before the U.S. military intervention. Given that many organizations are uniquely capable of conducting assessments, few understand what and how each other plan. The decision to pull out of Somalia was President Clinton's and this withdrawal from Mogadishu told a global narrative that the U.S. military could be deterred through asymmetrical means.[251] In Port-au-Prince, Haiti, only 18 days after 18 SOF operators

---

[251]Steven Metz and Douglas V. Johnson II, "Asymmetry and U.S. Military Strategy:

were killed in Somalia, this theme publically arrived in Haiti. In an attempt to deter U.S. Government intervention, armed factions repeated, "Remember Somalia!"[252]

Haiti

A review of Haiti finds that interagency and SOF planners lacked an understanding of the divergent cultures and organizations in Haiti. The roles and responsibilities of the civilian organization operating in Haiti differed from SOF. While interagency collaboration, on a grand scale, achieved the desired effects in Haiti, the goals, policies, procedures, and decision-making processes made planning disjointed. Planners did not receive training or education on the roles and responsibilities of contributing joint, interagency, and multinational organizations before arriving in Haiti. One military commander said that, "we didn't know the limits of our civilian agencies...We were ignorant about what the other agencies were doing."[253] In addition to the interagency process, intra-organizational understanding presented similar difficulties. Differences in training, education, and organizational cultures divided SOF and conventional military forces from achieving a common perspective on the problems and the solutions in Haiti.

The above analysis supports the hypothesis given that collaborative approaches will be necessary in the future. Additionally, interagency and SOF communities will require an evolution of organizational understanding of the goals, policies, procedures, and decision-making processes in order to enhance the capabilities of the U.S. Government. One way to do this is through

---

Definition, Background, and Strategic Concepts" (Monograph, U.S. Army War College, 2001), 4-5. According to Steven and Douglas, asymmetrical is "important to strategy, but not everything is asymmetrical." This monograph defines the term *asymmetrical* as acting, organizing, and thinking differently than opponents in order to maximize one's own advantages, exploit an opponent's weaknesses, attain the initiative, or gain greater freedom of action.

[252] Kretchik, Baumann, and Fishel, *Invasion, Intervention, "Intervasion": A Concise History*, 39.

[253] Hayes and Weatley, *Interagency and Political-Military Dimensions of Peace Operations: Haiti - A Case Study*, 17.

training and education programs. As the literature review highlighted, training and education programs contribute to the overall professional development of the U.S. Government, and are vital when working in divergent collaborative teams against irregular threats. The case studies underscore many of the challenges for the interagency and SOF communities during interventions in Somalia and Haiti in the 1990s. For strategic leaders, one serious challenge always includes the motive for intervention.

Summary

The motives for America's intervention in Somalia and Haiti varied from humanitarian issues in the war-torn Somalia to political fears triggered by the humanitarian struggles of Haitian "boat people" seeking refuge in the United States. Today, as it was in the early to mid-1990s, information is available globally in near real-time. In both Somalia and Haiti, we found that the media had vast effects on U.S. Government efforts. In Somalia, as drought led to famine, the media reported pictures of starving Somalis who would die from malnutrition if governments did not intervene. In Haiti, a global audience saw Haitians building sailboats from their deconstructed homes. These international news reports "pressured policymakers to take stronger action on behalf of civilians," by showing images from Somalia and Haiti on the news.[254]

As this thesis suggests, the nature of United States involvement in such humanitarian and security efforts will endure into the future. In 2008, the U.S. Army's Training and Doctrine Command published a pamphlet highlighting both the utility and dangers of the media stating, "[Today], the Internet and cable television have the ability, along with governments, to shape the perception of a global audience in near real-time. Every action conveys a message, and the interpretation of that message often carries from one audience to another in unintended and

---

[254]Strobel, *Late-Breaking Foreign Policy*, 193.

unpredictable ways."[255] As we have seen by examining these two case studies, it is necessary to understand the numerous variables influencing the efficiency and effectiveness of national security organizations. The conclusion will discuss three recommendations for the future of intervention in complex humanitarian intervention operations.

CONCLUSION

The compassion of the American people makes the United States unique. This places policymakers in difficult situations. This research addressed the relationship between interagency and special operations forces by analyzing United States intervention in OOTW, specifically in Somalia from 1992 - 1994 and Haiti from 1994 - 1995. This study showed that war and peace operations are alike in at least one respect; both are extensions of policy.[256] Within all military operations, tactical level leaders make decisions in real-time under the pressures of life-threatening combat. While authors are quick to play a revisionist role, these tactical level decisions do have value in educating and training a new class of future government leaders. As this research has shown, at a very fundamental level, the work of collective government lacks understanding. This lack of basic knowledge of national security organizations or specific country data, such as cultural sensitivities and societal construct, creates issues that become barriers to achieving the strategic aims. An understanding of the problem in depth can lead planners to develop a whole-of-government approach that ensures: 1) the U.S. Government is solving the right problem, and 2) it is doing so effectively utilizing all the capabilities resident throughout interagency organizations. As the evolution of warfare continues to shape and structure the style

---

[255]U.S. Army Training and Doctrine Command, *The United States Army Commander's Appreciation and Campaign Design,* 2008 (Fort Monroe, Virginia: Headquarters, United States Army 2008), 4.

[256]Kevin C. M. Benson and Christopher B. Thrash, "Declaring Victory: Planning Exit Strategies for Peace Operations, " *Parameters* XXVI (Autumn 1996).

of fighting (ways), it will be up to government leaders to determine the shape, size, and kind of

tools (the means) that support political aims (the ends). These tools will sharpen given sufficient

time and implementation of the aforementioned recommendations.[257] Without sharpening these

tools, our adversary will continue to adapt to a stagnant conduct in warfare.

While the preparation for war is dually expensive and burdensome, there is one important

part of it that costs little – the study of war.[258] As Field Marshall Slim recanted in his memoir,

"officers today can educate themselves at a relatively inexpensive benefit to the larger

organization; the country."[259] It may seem like a simple task to look at current events, or models,

and speculate how "hamstrung and broken" the interagency process is (or is not), but studying

historical models is more important to understanding change.[260] This interagency process sheds

light on broader issues that senior leaders can impact today, but one challenge is improving the

efficiency and effectiveness of national security organizations.

This research suggests improvements to the efficiency and effectiveness of national

security organizations would prove useful in unifying efforts across all the U.S. Government.

Military organizations and civilian organizations alike would benefit by emphasizing the utility of

the relationship between the military and civilian services. In 2010, the U.S. Government

Accountability Office stated that, "collaborative approaches to national security require a well-

trained workforce with the skills and expertise to integrate the government's diverse capabilities

---

[257]History shows that time is unfortunately not always on a planner's side.

[258]William Joseph Slim, *Defeat Into Victory: Battling Japan in Burma and India, 1942-1945*, (New York: Cooper Square Press: Distributed by National Book Network, 2000), 535.

[259]Ibid.

[260]As derived from economists March and Simon, Allison, Gouldner, Perrow, Doeringer and Piore, Williamson, Schumpeter, Nelson and Winter provide a useful introduction to the theory of organizational behavior and change. Richard R. Nelson and Sidney G. Winter, *An Evolution Theory of Economic Change* (Massachusetts: Belknap Press of Harvard University Press, 1985), 96-136.

and resources."[261] Additionally, Paul R. Pillar believes that "informal working relationships are as important as the formal ones," and that these relationships "are critical to each agency understanding the business and equities of the other agencies."[262]

Understanding organizational cultures is also largely important as new organizations bring with them more complexity to the process of collaboration. Bob Ulin says that federal organizations have "its own culture, operating procedures, jargon, and rules."[263] By rearranging some stovepipes between and within military and civilian organizations, the collective government would further benefit by emphasizing on the problems at hand instead of the competing organizational interests. This emphasis could provide opportunities to develop a shared understanding of the varied roles, responsibilities, authorities, and cultures of other governmental organizations. Frans P.B. Osinga continues this discourse by asserting, "If we don't communicate with the outside world – to gain information for knowledge and understanding…we die out and become non-discerning and uninterested part of the world."[264] This is an important point and shines light on reasons for collaborating with outside entities.

Strategic leaders have a role to play in advancing the practice of such comprehensive approaches. Pillar assesses that relationships between senior leaders of the Central Intelligence Agency (CIA) and Federal Bureau (FBI) has enabled employees to "learn more about the other

---

[261]U.S. Government Accountability Office, "Key Issues for Congressional Oversight of National Security Strategies, Organizations, Workforce, and Information Sharing, " http://www.gao.gov/assets/210/203867.pdf (accessed November 17, 2012), 2.; Pillar, *Terrorism and U.S. Foreign Policy*, 125.

[262]Pillar, *Terrorism and U.S. Foreign Policy*, 124.

[263]Ulin, "About Interagency Cooperation," 2.

[264]Frans P. B. Osinga, *Science, Strategy and War: The Strategic Theory of John Boyd*, Strategy and History (New York: Routledge, 2007), 83.

organization, and cross-assignments of personnel."[265] The FBI reserves a deputy chief position for a senior CIA operations officer, and similarly the CIA reserves a deputy chief position for a senior FBI special agency within their counter-terrorism center.[266] This collaboration shows organizational-level commitment to whole-of-government approaches that more broadly implemented could reverberate into a unified approach to solving complex issues.

This understanding mandates a breakdown in the current way organizations professionally develop their employees. Despite a lack of formalized processes between civilian and "operational" military units, organizations such as the DoD and the DoS, through education and training programs, highlight the value of unifying efforts by their participation in their collective approaches to education and training. While there was certainly a breakdown in collaboration in Somalia, the collaborative efforts in Haiti emphasize that the interagency process is not as "broken," as scholars from academia and government have stated. However, if the U.S. Government embraces countering irregular threats as an enduring task, it will require greater synergy between involved organizations, and ultimately an evolution in interagency collaboration.

---

[265]Pillar, *Terrorism and U.S. Foreign Policy*, 125.

[266]Ibid.

BIBLIOGRAPHY

Abizaid, John P., and John R, Wood. "Preparing for Peacekeeping: Military Training and the Peacekeeping Environment." *Special Warfare* 7, no. 2 (April 1994): 14-20.

Albright, Madeleine K. "Building a Consensus on International Peace-keeping." *U.S. Department of State Dispatch*, October 20, 1993.

Albright, Madeleine, and with Bill Woodward. *Madam Secretary*. New York, N.Y.: Miramax, 2003.

Allard, Kenneth. *Somalia Operations: Lessons Learned*. Washington D.C.: National Defense University Press, 1995.

Angstrom, Jan, and J.J. Widen. "Adopting a Recipe for Success: Modern Armed Forces and the Institutionalization of the Principles of War." *Comparative Politics* 31, no. 3 (July 2012): 263-85.

Baggott, Christopher L. "A Leap Into The Dark: Crisis Action Planning For Operation Restore Hope." MMAS Monograph, Command and General Staff College, 1996.

Belknap, Margaret H. "The CNN Effect: Strategic Enabler or Operational Risk?" *Parameters* XXXII (Autumn 2002): 100-114.

Benson, Kevin. "School of Advanced Military Studies: Commemorative History 1984-2009." SAMS.

Benson, Kevin C. M. and Christopher B. Thrash. "Declaring Victory: Planning Exit Strategies for Peace Operations." *Parameters* XXVI (Autumn 1996): 69-80.

Bentley, David and Robert Oakley. "Peace Operations: A Comparison of Somalia and Haiti." *National Defense University's Strategic Studies Forum transcript (Institute for National Strategic Studies)*, no. 30 (May 1995).

Bermeo, Sarah. "Clinton and Coercive Diplomacy: A Study of Haiti." Princeton, NJ: Princeton University, 2001.

Boisselle, James C. "Communicating the Vision: Psychological Operations in Operation Uphold Democracy," A657 (course) research paper. U.S. Army Command and General Staff College: Fort Leavenworth, KS, March 3, 1996.

Bolger, Daniel P. *Savage Peace: Americans at War in the 1990s*. California: Presidio, 1995.

Bolton, John R. "Wrong Turn in Somalia." *Foreign Affairs* 73, no. i (January-February 1994): 56-57.

Bowden, Mark. *Black Hawk Down: A Story of Modern War*. New York: Atlantic Monthly Press, 1999.

70

Brown, John S. *Kevlar Legions: The Transformation of the U.S. Army, 1989-2005*. Washington D.C.: Center of Military History United States Army, 2011.

Brown, Stewart Patrick and Kaysie. *Greater Than the Sum of Its Parts? Assessing "Whole of Government" approaches to Fragile States*. Washington D.C.: International Peace Academy, 2007.

Bureau of Political-Military Affairs. "Office of the Coordinator of the Foreign Policy Advisor Program (PM/POLAD)." U.S. Department of State. http://www.state.gov/t/pm/polad/ (accessed September 27, 2012).

Bush, George. "Address to the Nation on the Situation in Somalia." White House, Washington D.C., December 4, 1992. http://bushlibrary.tamu.edu/research/public_papers.php?id=5100&year=1992&month=12 (accessed January 31, 2013).

Campbell, David. "The Social and Cultural Impacts of the United States Occupation of the People of Haiti (1915-1934)," HIST 339 (course) research paper. Concordia University: Irvine CA, April 10, 2007. http://www.tchh.org/documents/Social%20and%20Cultural%20impacts%20of%20the%20US%20Occupation.pdf (accessed January 18, 2013).

Center for Army Lessons Learned. "U.S. Army Operations in Support of UNOSOM II." Fort Leavenworth, K.S.: U.S. Army Combined Arms Center.

Central Intelligence Agency. "Central America And Caribbean: Haiti." https://http://www.cia.gov/library/publications/the-world-factbook/maps/maptemplate_ha.html (accessed February 7, 2013).

———. "The World Factbook." Central Intelligence Agency. http://nodedge.com/ciawfb/ (accessed Feburary 7, 2013).

Cheong-Lum, Roseline Ng and Leslie Jermyn. *Cultures of the World: Haiti*. Tarrytown, NY: Marshall Cavendish Benchmark, 2005.

Christopher, Warren. *In the Stream of History: Shaping Foreign Policy for a New Era*. Stanford, CA: Stanford University Press, 1998.

Clapper, James R. "Unclassified Statement for the Record on the Worldwide Threats Assessment of the US Intelligence Community for the Senate Select Committee On Intelligence." Washington D.C.: Office of the Director of National Intelligence, 2012. www.intelligence.senate.gov/120131/clapper.pdf (accessed December 12, 2012).

Clinton, William J. "The President's Radio Address." The American Presidency Project. http://www.clintonlibrary.gov/assets/storage/Research-AV/audio/1994/DEC/PP_ROTP_RadioAddress_17Dec1994.mp3 (accessed February 5, 2013).

Couch, Dick. *The Warrior Elite: The Forging of Seal Class 228*. New York: Crown Publishers, 2001.

Countryman, Thomas. "National Security, Interagency Collaboration, and Lessons from SOUTHCOM and AFRICOM." In *The Subcommittee on National Security and Foreign Affairs House Committee Oversight and Government Reform*. Washington D.C.: U.S. Department of State, 2010. http://democrats.oversight.house.gov/images/stories/subcommittees/NS_Subcommittee/7.28.10_Interagency_Africom_and_southcom/Countryman_Statement.pdf (accessed July 28, 2012).

Davis, Geoffrey. "Interagency Reform: The Congressional Perspective." *Military Review* 88, no. 4 (July-August 2008): 2-6.

Department of Public Information. "United Nations Operation in Somalia II." United Nations. www.un.org/en/peacekeeping/missions/past/unosom2.htm (accessed January 5, 2013).

Dobbins, James F. "Haiti: A Case Study in Post Cold-War Peacekeeping." *Institute for the Study of Diplomacy* II, no. I (October 1995): 2-7. http://isd.georgetown.edu/files/ISDreport_Haiti_Dobbins.pdf (accessed March 10, 2013).

Dobbins, James, John G. McGinn, Keith Crane, Seth G. Jones, Rollie Lai, Andrew Rathmell, Rachel Swanger and Anga Timilsina. *America's Role in Nation-Building: From Germany to Iraq*. Santa Monica, CA: RAND, 2003.

Durant, Michael J., Steven Hartov and Robert L. Johnson. *The Night Stalkers: Top Secret Missions of the U.S. Army's Special Operations Aviation Regiment*. New York: G.P. Putnam's Sons, 2006.

Embassy of Haiti in Washington D.C.. "Key Dates in Haiti's History." Embassy of Haiti. http://www.haiti.org/images/stories/pdf/key_dates.pdf (accessed February 4, 2013).

Feickert, Andrew. "U.S. Special Operations Forces (SOF) Background and Issues for Congress." Washington D.C.: Congressional Research Service, 2012.

George, Alexander L., and Andrew Bennett. *Case Studies and Theory Development in the Social Sciences*. Cambridge, MA.: The MIT Press, 2005.

George Herbert Walker Bush Presidential Library. "NSC/DC Meeting List, 1989-1993." The George Bush Presidential Library and Museum. http://bushlibrary.tamu.edu/research/pdfs/nsc_and_dc_meetings_1989-1992-declassified.pdf (accessed December 18, 2012).

Gleiman, Jan Kenneth. "Operational Art and the Clash of Organizational Cultures: Postmortem on Special Operations as a Seventh Warfighting Function." MMAS Monograph, Command and General Staff College, 2011.

Goddard, Brent P. "Military Peacekeeping Operations in Haiti." Marine Corps University Command and Staff College, 1997.

Government Printing Office. *United States Code, 2006 Edition, Supplement 5, Title 10 - Armed Forces*. Washington D.C.: 2012. http://www.gpo.gov/fdsys/search/pagedetails.action?packageId=USCODE-2011-

title10&granuleId=USCODE-2011-title10-subtitleA-partI-chap6-sec167 (accessed
November 12, 2012)

Gray, Colin S. *War, Peace and International Relations: An Introduction to Strategic History.*
New York: Routledge, 2007.

Worldmark Encyclopedia of Nations. "Haiti." 2007. *Encyclopedia.com.*
http://www.encyclopedia.com/doc/1G2-2586700161.html (accessed March 14, 2013).

Halberstam, David. *War in a Time of Peace: Bush, Clinton, and the Generals.* New York, NY:
Simon and Schuster, 2001.

Hassig, Susan M. and Zawiah Abdul Latif. *Somalia.* New York: Marshall Cavendish Benchmark,
2008.

Hayes, Margaret Daly and Gary F. Weatley. "Interagency and Political-Military Dimensions of
Peace Operations: Haiti - A Case Study." Washington D.C.: National Defense University
Press, 1996.

Herring, George C. *From Colony to Superpower: U.S. Foreign Relations Since 1776.* New York:
Oxford University Press, 2011.

Herspring, Dale R. *The Pentagon and the Presidency: Civil-Military Relations from FDR to
George W. Bush.* Lawrence, KS: University Press of Kansas, 2005.

Johnson, Timothy D. *A Gallant Little Army: The Mexico City Campaign.* Kansas: The University
of Kansas 2007.

Jones, Garrett. "Working with the CIA." *Parameters* XXXI, (Winter 2001-02): 28-39,
http://www.carlisle.army.mil/usawc/Parameters/Articles/01winter/jones.htm.

Kiras, James. *Special Operations and Strategy: From World War II to the War on Terrorism.*
New York: Routledge, 2006.

Klein, Kimberly Nastasi. "Establishing U.S. Africa Command." Project on National Security
Reform.
http://old.pnsr.org/web/page/932/sectionid/579/pagelevel/3/parentid/590/interior.asp
(accessed February 3, 2013).

Kretchik, Walter E., Robert F. Baumann and John T. Fishel. *Invasion, Intervention,
"Intervasion": A Concise History of the U.S. Army in Operation Uphold Democracy.*
Fort Leavenworth, K.S.: U.S. Army Command and General Staff College Press, 1998.

Lake, Anthony. "Defining Missions, Setting Deadlines." Prepared remarks to George Washington
University, Washington D.C., March 6, 1996.
http://www.defense.gov/speeches/speech.aspx?speechid=898 (accessed January 31,
2013).

Lewis, John P. "Oral History Interviews: Operation Uphold Democracy." edited by Cynthia L.
Hayden. Port-au-Prince, Haiti: Christopher Clark.

Meredith, Martin. *The Fate of Africa: From the Hopes of Freedom to the Heart of Despair: A History of Fifty Years of Independence*. New York: Public Affairs, 2005.

Metz, Helen Chapin. "Dominican Republic and Haiti: Country Studies." Washington, D.C.: Library of Congress, 2001. http://lcweb2.loc.gov/frd/cs/httoc.html (accessed January 2, 2013).

Metz, Steven and Douglas V. Johnson II. "Asymmetry and U.S. Military Strategy: Definition, Background, and Strategic Concepts." Carlisle, PA: U.S. Army War College, 2001. http://www.au.af.mil/au/awc/awcgate/ssi/asymetry.pdf (accessed August 3, 2012).

Mitchell, Eric I. "Oral History Interviews: Operation Uphold Democracy." edited by Cynthia L. Hayden. Port-au-Prince, Haiti: Christopher Clark.

Montgomery, Thomas M. *United States Forces, Somalia After Action Report and Historical Overview: The United States Army in Somalia, 1992-1994*. Washington D.C.: Center of Military History, 2003. http://www.history.army.mil/html/documents/somalia/SomaliaAAR.pdf (accessed November 26, 2012).

Moore, Robin. *The Green Berets*. New York: Crown Publishers, 1965.

Nelson, Richard R., and Sidney G. Winter. *An Evolutionary Theory of Economic Change*. Massachusetts: Belknap Press of Harvard University Press, 1985.

North Central Association of Colleges and Schools. "Higher Learning Commission: U.S. Army Command and General Staff College." The Higher Learning Commission. http://www.ncahlc.org/component/com_directory/Action,ShowBasic/Itemid,/instid,2036/ (accessed December 6, 2012).

Office of the Historian. "National Security Act of 1947." U.S. Department of State. http://history.state.gov/milestones/1945-1952/NationalSecurityAct (accessed September 27, 2012).

O'Neil IV, John E. "The Interagency Process – Analysis and Reform Recommendations." Carlisle Barracks, PA: U.S. Army War College, 2006. http://www.strategicstudiesinstitute.army.mil/pdffiles/ksil445.pdf (accessed July 29, 2012).

Osinga, Frans P. B. *Science, Strategy and War: The Strategic Theory of John Boyd Strategy and History*. New York: Routledge, 2007.

Otunnu, Olara A. and Michael W. Doyle. *Peacemaking and Peacekeeping for the New Century*. Lanham: Rowman & Littlefield Publishers, 1998.

Pattee, Phillip G. "Special Operations Forces and Nonstate Actors in Operation Uphold Democracy: A Case Study." U.S. Army Command and General Staff College, 1996.

Peterson, Scott. *Me Against My Brother: At War in Somalia, Sudan, and Rwanda: A Journalist Reports from the Battlefields of Africa*. New York: Routledge, 2000.

Pillar, Paul R. *Terrorism and U.S. Foreign Policy*. Washington D.C.: Brookings Institution Press, 2003.

Pine, Art and John M. Broder. "U.S. Faults Intelligence in Failed Somalia Raid." *Los Angeles Times*, August 31, 1993. http://articles.latimes.com/1993-08-31/news/mn-29737_1_clinton-administration (accessed February 1, 2013).

Ploch, Lauren. "Africa Command: U.S. Strategic Interests and the Role of the U.S. Military in Africa." Washington D.C.: Congressional Research Service, 2011.

Preeg, Ernest H. *The Haitian Dilemma: A Case Study in Demographics, Development, and U.S. Foreign Policy*. Washington, D.C.: Center for Strategic and International Studies, 1996. http://haitipolicy.org/Dilemma.pdf (accessed February 17, 2013).

Project on National Security Reform. "Forging a New Shield: Executive Summary." PNSR. http://0183896.netsolhost.com/site/wp-content/uploads/2011/12/pnsr-forging_exec-summary_12-2-08.pdf (accessed March 10, 2013).

Ricks, Charles. *Special Operations Forces Interagency Counterterrorism Reference Manual*. 2nd ed. Tampa, Florida: Joint Special Operations University, 2011.

Rothkopf, David. *Running the World: The Inside Story of the National Security Council and the Architects of American Power*. New York: Public Affairs, 2005.

Runzi, Clay O. "Transforming the National Security Council: Interagency Authority, Organization, Doctrine." MSSD Monograph, U.S. Army War College, 2007.

Salter, Margaret S. "Training for Operations Other Than War (Stability Operations): Front End Analysis." www.dtic.mil/cgi-bin/GetTRDoc?AD=ADA323247 (accessed July 31, 2012)

Schmidt, Hans. *The U.S. Occupation of Haiti*. New Brunswick, N.J.: Rutgers University Press, 1971.

Schulz, Donald E. and Gabriel Marcella. "Reconciling the Irreconcilable: The troubled outlook for U.S. policy toward Haiti." Carlisle Barracks, PA, U.S. Army War College, 1994.

School of Advanced Military Studies. "School of Advanced Military Studies: Trifold." SAMS. http://usacac.army.mil/cac2/cgsc/Events/SAMS25th/SAMSTri-fold.pdf (accessed December 3, 2012).

Sharkey, Jacqueline E. "The Shallow End of the Pool?" *American Journalism Review*. (1994). http://www.ajr.org/article.asp?id=1580 (accessed February 18, 2013).

Shay, Shaul. *Somalia between Jihad and Restoration*. New Brunswick, N.J.: Transaction Publishers, 2010.

Short, Edward C. "Oral History Interviews: Operation Uphold Democracy." edited by Cynthia L. Hayden. Port-au-Prince, Haiti: Thomas G. Ziek.

Siegel, Adam B. *The Intervasion of Haiti*. Alexandria, VA: Center for Naval Analysis, 1996.

Slim, William Joseph. *Defeat Into Victory: Battling Japan in Burma and India, 1942-1945*. New York: Cooper Square Press, 2000.

"Somalia, Somaliland, and Puntland." Encyclopedia Britannica. http://www.britannica.com/EBchecked/media/124811/The-Republic-of-Somalia-experienced-fragmentation-in-the-1990s-the (accessed February 13, 2013).

Special Operations. "The CIA in Somalia, 1993." Special Operations. http://www.specialoperations.com/Operations/Restore_Hope/CIA.htm (accessed December 15, 2012).

Stanley, Bruce. "Wargames, Training, and Decision-Making: Increasing the Experience of Army Leaders." MMAS Monograph, Command and General Staff College, 1999.

Stephanopoulos, George. *All Too Human: A Political Education*. Boston, MA: Little, Brown, 1999.

Stewart, Richard W. *The United States Army in Somalia, 1992-1994*. Washington D.C.: U.S. Army Center of Military History: U.S. Government Publishing Office 2002.

Strobel, Warren P. *Late-Breaking Foreign Policy: The News Media's Influence on Peace Operations*. Washington D.C.: United States Institute of Peace, 1997.

Sullivan, Michael L. "Oral History Interviews: Operation Uphold Democracy." edited by Cynthia L. Hayden. Port-au-Prince, Haiti: Charles Cureton.

The Observer. "Reluctant Warrior." The Guardian. http://www.guardian.co.uk/world/2001/sep/30/usa.afghanistan (accessed January 5, 2013).

Tierney, Geoffrey C. Davis and John F. "The Need for Interagency Reform: Congressional Perspective and Efforts." *InterAgency Journal* 3, no. 1 (Winter 2012): 3-7.

Tierney, John F. U.S. Congress. House. Committee on Committee on Oversight and Government Reform: Subcommittee on National Security and Foreign Affairs. *National Security, Interagency Collaboration, and Lessons from SOUTHCOM and AFRICOM*. 111th Cong., 2d sess., July 28, 2010.

Tovo, Kenneth E. "Special Forces' Missions Focus For The Future." MMAS Monograph, Command and General Staff College, 1995.

Tucker, David and Christopher J. Lamb. *United States Special Operations Forces*. New York: Columbia University Press, 2007.

Turabian, Kate L. *A Manual for Writers of Term Papers, Theses, and Dissertations*. 7th ed. Chicago: University of Chicago Press, 2007.

U.S. Army Training and Doctrine Command. *The United States Army Commander's Appreciation and Campaign Design*. Fort Monroe, Virginia: 2008.

U.S. Census Bureau. "Table 165-6. Physicians by Sex and Specialty: 1980-1992." U.S. Census. http://www.census.gov/compendia/statab/2012/tables/12s0165.pdf (accessed February 16, 2013).

U.S. Congress. "National Security Act of 1947 (Public law 253, 80th Congress, July 26, 1947, 61 Stat. 495) as amended to January 8, 1952, and including the National Security Act amendments of 1949, Public law 216, 81st Congress, August 10, 1949, 63 Stat. 578." edited by 80th Cong., iv, 31 p. Washington D.C.: U.S. Government Printing Office, 1952.

U.S. Congress. House. Committee on House Armed Services Committee. *Skelton, Davis Introduce Groundbreaking Interagency Reform Legislation.* 111th Cong., 2nd sess., 2010. http://democrats.armedservices.house.gov/index.cfm/2010/9/skelton--davis-introduce-groundbreaking-interagency-reform-legislation (accessed October 23, 2012).

————. House. *Offices of the Fourth Congressional District of Kentucky to Remain Open to Serve and Assist Constituents.* Office of the Clerk of the House of Representatives. http://clerk.house.gov/about/press/08012012_01.aspx (accessed February 3, 2013).

U.S. Congress. Senate. "Review of the Circumstances Surrounding the Ranger Raid on October 3-4, 1993 in Mogadishu." In *Committee on Armed Services.* Washington D.C.: United States Senate, 1995. http://www.fas.org/irp/congress/1995_rpt/mogadishu.pdf (accessed December 3, 2012).

————. "Interagency Personnel Rotation Act of 2011." ed. by Senate of the United States, S1268. Washington D.C.: Congressional Record, 2011. http://www.govtrack.us/congress/bills/112/s1268 (accessed November 2, 2012).

U.S. Department of Defense. Irregular Warfare Joint Operating Concept Version 1.0. Office of the Secretary of Defense. Washington D.C.: 2007. www.fas.org/irp/doddir/dod/iw-joc.pdf (accessed January 31, 2013).

————. Joint Publication 1-02: *Department of Defense Dictionary of Military and Associated Terms.* Washington D.C.: 2010.

————. Joint Publication 3-0: *Joint Operations.* Washington D.C.: 2011.

————. Joint Publication 3-05: *Special Operations.* Washington D.C.: 2011.

————. Joint Publication 3-07: *Joint Doctrine for Military Operations Other Than War.* Washington D.C.: 1995.

————. Joint Publication 3-07: *Stability Operations.* Washington D.C.: 2011.

————. Joint Publication 3-07.3: *Peace Operations.* Washington D.C.: 2007.

————. Joint Publication 3-08: *Interagency Coordination During Joint Operations.* Washington D.C.: 1996.

U.S. Department of State. "U.S. Relations with Haiti." Bureau of Western Hemisphere Affairs. http://www.state.gov/r/pa/ei/bgn/1982.htm (accessed February 4, 2012).

U.S. Department of State Dispatch. "Background Notes: Haiti." Bureau of Public Affairs. http://dosfan.lib.uic.edu/ERC/briefing/dispatch/1995/html/Dispatchv6no24.html (accessed February 4, 2013).

U.S. Department of the Army. *Field Manual 3-06, Appendix C: Operations in Somalia: Applying the Urban Operational Framework to Support and Stability.* Washington D.C.: 2006.

U.S. Diplomacy. "Diplomats in Harms Way." http://www.usdiplomacy.org/history/service/jamesbishop.php (accessed February 1, 2013).

U.S. Government. "Accountability Office. Key Issues for Congressional Oversight of National Security Strategies, Organizations, Workforce, and Information Sharing." Washington D.C.: Government Accountability Office, 2009, GAO-09-904SP. http://www.gao.gov/assets/210/203867.pdf (accessed October 12, 2012).

———. "Improving Planning, Training, and Interagency Coordination Could Strengthen DOD's Efforts in Africa." Washington D.C.: Government Accountability Office, 2010, GAO-10-794. http://www.gao.gov/assets/310/307759.pdf (accessed October 2, 2012).

———. "An Overview of Professional Development Activities Intended to Improve Interagency Collaboration." Washington D.C.: Government Accountability Office, 2010, GAO-11-108.

———. "Nonproliferation: Agencies Could Improve Information Sharing and End-Use Monitoring on Unmanned Aerial Vehicle Exports." Washington D.C.: Government Accountability Office, 2012, GAO-12-536.

U.S. Joint Special Operations University. "2011 JSOU Publications." Joint Special Operations Education. https://jsou.socom.mil/Pages/2011JSOUPublications.aspx (accessed October 3, 2012).

U.S. Special Operations Command. "About USSOCOM." USSOCOM. http://www.socom.mil/Pages/AboutUSSOCOM.aspx (accessed October 2, 2012).

U.S. Special Operations Command. *U.S. Special Operations Command Fact Book 2013.* Tampa, Florida: Headquarters, 2012.

Ulin, Bob. "About Interagency Cooperation." *InterAgency Essay* no. 10-01, (2010).

United Nations. "Somalia - UNOSOM I: Background." United Nations. www.un.org/en/peacekeeping/missions/past/unosom1backgr2.html.

———. "Somalia - UNOSOM II Mandate." United Nations. http://www.un.org/en/peacekeeping/missions/past/unosom2mandate.html (accessed January 11, 2013).

United Nations Security Council. "Resolution 751 (1992): as of 24 April 1992." edited by United Nations. New York: UN Publications, 1992.

Walzer, Michael. "The Argument about Humanitarian Intervention." *Dissent* 49, no. 1 (Winter 2002): 29-37.

———. *Just and Unjust Wars: A Moral Argument with Historical Illustrations*. 4th ed. New York: Basic Books, 2006.

Watts, Clint, Jacob Shapiro and Vahid Brown. *Al-Qa'ida's (Mis)Adventures in the Horn of Africa*. West Point, New York: Combating Terrorism Center, 2007.

Weiss, Thomas G. "Overcoming the Somalia Syndrome - "Operation Rekindle Hope?"." *Global Governance* I (1995): 171-187, http://heinonline.org/HOL/LandingPage?collection=journals&handle=hein.journals/glog ol&div=17&id=&page= (accessed August 12, 2012).

Wilder, Mathew. "Achieving Unity of Effort." *InterAgency Journal* 3, no. 1 (Winter 2011): 40-46.

White House. "Fact Sheet: Procedures Implementing Section 1022 of the National Defense Authorization Act for Fiscal Year 2012." http://www.whitehouse.gov/sites/default/files/ndaa_fact_sheet.pdf (accessed March 13, 2013).